YEHUDI G... at the Garden Hospital, London, and father of three children. He graduated in South Africa and was later awarded the Royal College of Obstetricians Research Fellowship in London. His biochemical research into foetal well-being has led to the publication of many scientific papers. A pioneer in the field of natural active birth in the UK, Yehudi Gordon is known for introducing a homelike, supportive atmosphere into hospital. He has been involved with the use of water for labour and birth since 1982. He was an integral member of the Active Birth Movement and has created a unique ante and postnatal programme with the emphasis on self help. He is the co-author, with Janet Balaskas of *The Encyclopaedia of Pregnancy and Birth* (1987).

JANET BALASKAS is a pioneer and innovator in the field of childbirth education and maternity care. She introduced the use of upright birth postures both in Great Britain and abroad and first coined the phrase 'Active Birth' and founded the Active Birth Movement in 1982.

She lectures internationally and is a well-known campaigner for women's rights in childbirth. She is the author of several books, including *New Active Birth* and *Natural Pregnancy* and is co-author with Yehudi Gordon of *The Encyclopedia of Pregnancy and Birth*.

Janet Balaskas lives and works in London with her four children and her husband Keith Brainin. They run the International Active Birth Centre, which is also a resource and education centre for water birth. Together they have helped to facilitate the wide availability of water birth services throughout the UK and in other countries.

Other books by the authors
New Active Birth, Janet Balaskas, Unwin Hyman Paperbacks
Encyclopaedia of Pregnancy and Birth, Janet Balaskas and Yehudi Gordon,
Macdonald Orbis
New Life, The Exercise Book for Childbirth, Janet Balaskas, Sidgwick &
Jackson
The Active Birth Partner's Handbook, Sidgwick & Jackson
Natural Pregnancy, Janet Balaskas, Sidgwick & Jackson
Yoga for Pregnancy, audio cassette and booklet, Janet Balaskas, Active Birth
Centre Publication

Relaxing in water two weeks after birth

WATER BIRTH

Janet Balaskas
Yehudi Gordon

Thorsons
An Imprint of HarperCollins*Publishers*

Don

Thorsons
An Imprint of HarperCollins*Publishers*
77–85 Fulham Palace Road,
Hammersmith, London W6 8JB

Published by Thorsons 1992
First published by Unwin Paperbacks,
an imprint of Unwin Hyman Limited, 1990
10 9 8 7 6 5 4

A catalogue record for this book
is available from the British Library

ISBN 0 7225 2788 8

Printed in Great Britain by
Woolnough Bookbinding Limited,
Irthlingborough, Northamptonshire

For preparation, workshops and information about
Water Birth or Water Pools parents and professionals
can contact:

The Active Birth Centre, 55 Dartmouth Park Road,
London NW5 1SL
Telephone: 071 267 3006 Fax: 071 267 5368

Contents

Acknowledgements

We thank the courageous mothers who have used water for labour and birth. This was made possible by the pioneering midwives and obstetricians who introduced the use of water pools at home and in hospital and have thus opened a new dimension of choice and freedom for women.

Thanks to our families for their support during the writing of this book. We are especially grateful to the people who appear in the photographs and to Gena Naccache for her sensitive photography. Thanks also to her husband Adrian for his help in the darkroom and to Lucy Su for her beautiful illustrations. Thank you to Ann Herreboudt and Deborah Quinn-Scoggins for their advice on baby swimming and for the photographs which illustrate this section. These photographs were taken during a baby swim class at the Britannia Leisure Centre, Hackney, and we would like to thank the Centre and its staff for kindly allowing us to use the facilities.

We also thank Stephen Russell for the baby massage, Caroline Holliday, Gill Driver, Suzie Kent and Alice Charlwood for typing the manuscript and Clare Ford at Unwin Hyman for her encouragement. Last, but not least, we thank Keith Brainin for his ingenious birth pools which have helped to change Water Birth from a dream to a reality.

The authors and publishers would also like to thank Michel Odent and Arkana for the extract from *Water and Sexuality* (Arkana, 1990), Michel Odent, and Heathcote Williams and Jonathan Cape Ltd for the extracts from *Whale Nation* (Jonathan Cape, 1988), ©Heathcote Williams, and *Falling for a Dolphin* (Jonathan Cape, 1988), ©Heathcote Williams.

> Midwives who aid
> Women who do
> Fathers who are

Foreword
Janet Balaskas

In recent decades, women all over the world have been discovering that they do not have to succumb to obstetric control and are finding new ways both to empower themselves during pregnancy and to give birth autonomously. Wherever this occurs, birth becomes less complicated, the rate of intervention decreases dramatically and fewer babies need to be rescued. While the benefits of modern obstetrics, are clear for complicated births, the hazards of routinely disturbing the delicately-tuned physiological processes of birth are now increasingly obvious.

Today, our concern is to understand more deeply what a mother needs to access her instinctive power and potential and then to create the best possible environment and climate to help her to give birth naturally. This book is about how the power of water can be used to benefit mother, father and baby throughout the primal period from conception, labour and birth, until the end of infancy.

During the past few years, there has been a wave of excitement flowing through the 'birth world', as the use of water birth pools has rapidly increased. At the Active Birth Centre in 1987, my husband, Keith Brainin, designed an ingenious portable water pool which could be easily transported in the back of a car. This meant that water could potentially be introduced into any birthing environment. Since then, due to popular demand, more than 40 birth pools, both permanently installed and portable, have been produced. These are in constant use throughout the UK and even further afield. They are used in a variety of settings, within the NHS and privately, at home and in hospitals.

During my own four pregnancies, I found both swimming and yoga indispensable. Like many women, when I first saw photographs of mothers in Moscow labouring, giving birth and breastfeeding under water in the 60s, I was intrigued and very attracted to the possibility.

My first experience of the power of water to aid a birth was in 1978, when my third child Iasonas was born at home. It was a hot summer's day and in the early stages of the labour I went swimming with my midwife at the local pool. Later on, the feeling and memory of the water stayed with me. I could close my eyes at any point and remember the caress of the water on my skin and relax more deeply into the opening of my body. It was an extraordinary experience and Iasonas was consequently born easily.

When my son Theo came along in 1988, ten years had passed since Iasonas's birth and this time I could be considered as 'high risk'. I was 42, rhesus negative and had had surgery on my uterus three years previously. Besides, it was obvious that he was an exceptionally large baby – as it turned out he weighed 11lb (5kg) at birth. It seemed to me that I had a number of very good reasons to choose a home birth where I could have a water pool and the privacy, attention and familiar home comforts I needed to maximise my chances of a normal birth, as well as the reassurance of obstetric help nearby if I needed it. Michel Odent delivered Theo and for feminine company I had my beautiful daughter Kim (then 12 years old) and my dear friend Carole Eliott, who is an experienced mother and grandmother and a very gifted midwife. As if all that is not blessing enough, Keith had transformed our bedroom into the ideal environment for Theo's birth.

In the corner under the eaves by the window, there was a circular pool filled with calm blue water. Beside the pool there was a fire burning in the hearth and just enough space in front of the bed to move around in comfort.

The night before labour started we filled the pool. I spent several hours in the water, bathed in the light of the full moon shining through the window. I felt that the water was helping me to draw on all the energy and resources I would need. I slept soundly and awoke empowered, relaxed, confident and ready for the birth.

Towards evening, labour started in earnest. Typical of a fourth birth, contractions were very intense and painful from the outset. Like most women I could hardly wait to enter the calm pool in the darkened corner of the room. Once I did, the effect was transformative. My cumbersome body became light and movement from one position to another was easy. It was a tremendous relief to let go of the need to carry my weight. The intense pain at the peak of contractions was still there, but it was much easier to get through them. Most of all, the change of consciousness was remarkable. My mind stopped thinking – I was in a timeless ocean – completely surrendered to the rhythms of the labour.

It seemed like only minutes had passed, when I heard Michel suggesting that I should leave the pool. In fact, I had been in the water for about two hours. As Theo was so large, it was wiser to make the most of the help of gravity for the birth. Then, with Keith supporting me from behind in a standing squat, Theo was born beside the fire. Despite his size, neither of us sustained any injuries, and thanks to the softening effects of the water, there was no tear.

After the birth, all of us were in an ecstatic state for days, as is common after such an experience. Theo is now 18 months old and we have enjoyed a special closeness in water in the bath at home and also in the swimming pool throughout his infancy.

In addition to my own experience, it has been tremendously inspiring to hear the reports of other women who have enjoyed using water during labour and birth. Most of them are euphoric about the way it helped them, and their enthusiasm is shared by many of the midwives and doctors who were present. Over the years many new questions have been raised about the practicalities and the potential benefits and hazards involved in using a water pool. At the Centre we are contacted almost daily by parents and midwives seeking information.

In addressing these queries, I was inspired to write *Water Birth* with Yehudi Gordon as a guide for parents and professionals. It is our sincere hope that this book will help to make the benefits of water during labour and birth widely available as an option in the future and that parents will be inspired to make more use of water during pregnancy and after the birth.

Janet Balaskas
1990

Foreword
Yehudi Gordon

The idea of writing a book on the influence of water in the primal period from conception, birth and into infancy has inspired me to explore my own feelings about our relationship with water. My memories of childhood in South Africa are replete with images of swimming in pools, rivers and in the warm Indian Ocean. In 1970, when my wife Wendy was six months pregnant with our son Nick, we flew to Mozambique and went scuba-diving amongst the coral, fish, sharks and porpoises in the sea off Bazaruto Island. Little did I dream then that within ten years I would visit Michel Odent in Pithiviers and observe a birth pool in use on the labour ward. I helped Michel to carry the new pool into the hospital and on my return to London my immediate priority was to install a water pool in our labour suite. It is one of the most important, beneficial decisions I have made as an obstetrician.

Water has added an extra dimension to the resources which are available to support women and their families during one of the most important events of their lives. The power of the water pool in helping to relieve the pain of labour and birth has led to the disappearance of Pethidine, a narcotic drug used to decrease pain, from our labour ward since 1982. Water has therefore played a major part in making labour safer and ensuring that mothers and babies are awake and alert to experience the moment of birth and to enjoy their first few hours together.

Water has also profoundly influenced the midwives and obstetricians working in the Birthing Unit in the Hospital of St. John and St. Elizabeth. The pool has a soothing and calming effect on everyone involved in labour and birth and helps us to enjoy our vocation. Water acts as a natural extension to the skills midwives have used for millennia, and enhances the traditional warm, sympathetic and compassionate relationship between mother and midwife. If the labour is long, or the contractions become overwhelming, water provides a safe but powerful medium to encourage the mother to access her deepest resources and diminish her fear. In most labours this is sufficient to avoid technological intervention and the water pool is a new ally for the midwife at a crucial time when obstetrics seems to be taking over and controlling birth.

The first pool installed in our hospital was shallow and narrow and we soon realised that the depth and width of the water was crucial. The mother must be able to submerge completely to make maximum use of the bouyancy and anti-gravitational effect of the water. The pool should not be too big, so that the mother feels safe, secure, enclosed and protected. Earthy colours and low lighting in the room help this feeling.

The vast majority of women in labour use the water for relaxation and pain relief whilst only a minority choose to remain in the pool for the birth. Women are spending more and more time in the water, particularly after the birth, as they relax and welcome the new baby. The amazing power of water helps the newborn baby through the transition between life in the womb and life on land. During the following months this experience is often extended to bathing together at home and learning to swim.

Human beings evolved from the sea and we retain the internal sea inside each of the cells of our body. Although the healing power of water has been appreciated for millennia, its use in labour is relatively new. I am grateful to the two pioneers in waterbirth, Igor Tcharkovsky and Michel Odent, for their courage and foresight in introducing the use of water at the time of birth. It is a source of regret to me that when my three children were born, water was not available to them, but I am pleased that this resource is now available to a new generation of mothers and babies. It will certainly encourge the natural flow of energy during the primal period and may have a profound long-term effect on both mother and baby.

Yehudi Gordon
1990

1
Why Water?

At the present time we are witnessing an unusual and unprecedented phenomenon in human behaviour. For the first time, women in many different countries are deliberately choosing an aquatic environment for labour and birth. Water has been used in labour throughout history and midwives know that a warm bath may help in a long or difficult birth. With the exception of a tribe of South Pacific islanders who are said to give birth in shallow sea water, there is no recorded history of human mothers giving birth intentionally in water prior to the 1960s.

There are legends and stories which have reached us by word of mouth of birth practices in water amongst the Maoris, the American Indians near Panama and the ancient Greeks. It is also said that some priests in ancient Egypt were born in water, although there is no documented evidence to substantiate these legends.

And yet, the idea of relaxing during labour in a pool of warm water is very appealing to increasing numbers of women all over the world. Many women feel a strong attraction to water in labour. While most women prefer to leave the pool at the end of labour, some express a natural and instinctive desire to remain in water to give birth. And yet, as far as we know, birth in water is not common amongst primitive women who live close to nature. We may ask ourselves why this new phenomenon is arising in the more highly industrialised countries where modern obstetric maternity practices are most deeply established.

At present, childbirth practices are changing radically. Many parents and professionals are disillusioned with routine obstetric management of labour and birth. While obstetric technology provides a wonderful safety net when problems arise, the risks, disadvantages and consequences of disturbing the normal physiology of the birth process as a routine, are becoming more obvious to all concerned. The 'cascade' of interventions that often follow when obstetric procedures are used inappropriately, has been seen all over the world to lead to an increase in the number of forceps deliveries and caesarian sections (1). Consequently, many women today are rejecting the option of highly technological childbirth and choosing to give birth actively. There is now widespread recognition of the disadvantages of confining mothers to the supine or semi-reclining position during labour (2) (see table on page 29).

When observing how women behave when they are free to be mobile and instinctive it has been possible to learn much more about the normal physiology of the birth process (see page 28). The important role that gravity has to play during birth is being rediscovered and more widely understood (3).

We are also learning that humans share with other mammals a need for seclusion, darkness and privacy when giving birth (4). When a woman gives birth in a safe environment which has these characteristics, such as at home or in an intimate homelike hospital setting, the physiological process is almost always more efficient. All mammals need this privacy and security in order to secrete the hormones which facilitate the birth process and women are no exception (5) (see page 16). In a water pool the mother's sense of privacy is increased. She has her own small space in which she can relax and surrender to the involuntary contractions which open her womb and expel her baby. She is helped and protected by the water and has more control over her body, greater freedom to move and less possibility of being disturbed or distracted.

The relief from pain and greater privacy are two compelling factors which attract modern women to the use of water for birth. While it is important to approach birth without a fixed idea of how the baby will be born, another important person to consider is the newborn child. Throughout pregnancy the baby is an aquatic creature. At birth a dramatic change occurs and the newborn enters the world of gravity, breathes air and feels the cooler temperatures of the atmosphere. For the baby, birth is a momentous, but sometimes hazardous, experience. Leaving the security of the womb, the baby is squeezed by muscular contractions and pushed through the narrow passage of the birth canal. Once outside the new sensations of body weight, sight, sound and smell bombard the senses. Learning to breathe, separating from the pulsing cord and the unconditional nuturing of the placenta, finding the breast and sucking for the first time, these are all part of the dramatic transition that takes place when the baby leaves the shelter of the mother's body.

We know that babies are highly sensitive and impressionable at this time and that they can be affected for life by these early experiences. For this reason many mothers and fathers are attracted to the possibility of birth into water as a way to make the experience as easy as possible for the baby. The baby is born into the familiar medium of water. The temperature is similar to body temperature and the first sensations of light, touch and sound are softened. First contact between parents and baby can take place with mother, baby and sometimes father as well, still in the pool. The baby's entry into the atmosphere can be more gradual and gentle.

The use of water for labour and birth is understandably popular amongst women giving birth at home where it is generally easier to arrange to have the right facilities. Many hospitals are also keen to provide a water pool for use during labour in order to help mothers who wish to have a natural birth, to avoid the need for intervention. The presence of a water pool in a hospital provides a refuge from intrusive sounds, lighting and other disturbances, while allowing the security of obstetric back-up should a problem arise.

In pregnancy and also after birth, bathing in water offers a useful and very pleasurable way to exercise, soothe, calm, relax and enhance health and wellbeing. It is a wonderful activity for infants and can enrich their enjoyment of life, improve sleep and stimulate healthy development.

THE HISTORY OF THE USE OF WATER FOR CHILDBIRTH

The idea of creating an aquatic environment for birth was pioneered by the Soviet researcher and swimming instructor Igor Tjarkovsky in Moscow in the 1960s.

His early research centred around the ability of mammals to adapt to an aquatic environment (see page 20). He discovered that a variety of mammals could be trained to give birth and nurture their young under water, and observed that water made the birth easier and enhanced the development of the newborn. When his daughter was born prematurely he created a water environment for her as a replacement for the womb. Although the doctors had previously doubted that she would survive, she made a remarkable recovery and consequently spent a great deal of her infancy in water accompanying her father to the swimming pool. When Tjarkovsky observed her unusually fast development compared to her peers, he realised that water had great potential to enhance infant life and became interested in human birth under water. He installed a glass tank in the bathroom of his home, deep enough for a woman in labour to be almost fully immersed in water. Over the years he has assisted many mothers to give birth in the tank. Some of these early water births were recorded photographically and published in the West where they aroused a great deal of interest (6). Women who saw them were intrigued by the beautiful sight of a naked mother holding her newborn baby in her arms as the first sucking took place under water.

In the late 1960s the French obstetrician Frederick Leboyer first introduced the idea of immersing the newborn baby in a warm bath immediately after birth. His concern was to make the baby's transition from the womb into the world as gentle and easy as possible. The book *Birth Without Violence* and the film *A Child is Born* showed Leboyer gently and slowly bathing a newborn baby in water immediately after birth (7)(8).

The film shows the baby smiling less than one hour after birth with a look of blissful serenity on its face. The impact of this film at the time was startling and began a welcome trend towards more gentle births all over the world; focusing attention on the experiences, sensitivity and needs of the baby. His later film *The Art of Breathing* uses visual and sound images of water as a poetic metaphor for the tides of labour, starting with a trickling stream and ending with strong river currents and huge tidal waves of the sea preceding the baby's first cries.

The pioneer of the use of water for labour and birth in the West is the French Obstetrician Michel Odent. When he first introduced a water pool into the maternity unit at the hospital in Pithiviers in France, he was primarily looking for a way to help mothers to cope with pain and avoid intervention during labour without using drugs. In the 1970s he created the now famous 'primitive' birth room at the General Hospital in Pithiviers, France. The room bore no resemblance to a conventional hospital delivery room and was designed to allow the mother in labour freedom to follow her own instincts without being disturbed or distracted. The colours of the simple furnishings in the room were all dark or earthy tones, and heavy curtains ensured an atmosphere of semi-darkness. The only piece of furniture was a low platform covered with soft cushions, so that the mother could make herself comfortable in any position she chose. In 1977 Odent installed a simple round inflatable pool in an adjoining room, so that mothers could choose to lie in warm water (9). Over the next five or six years, thousands of women used the pool during labour. It was especially useful when labour was painful or for very long labours. Entering the warm water often helped the mother to reach full dilation quickly. Sometimes the mother preferred to remain in the pool for the birth and by 1983 a hundred births had occurred under water.

Odent observed that the majority of mothers chose to leave the pool for the actual birth. He emphasised that the pool was offered to facilitate labour and not with any conscious intention to encourage birth under water. Sometimes, however, birth spontaneously occurred in the pool and Odent realised that there were no special risks attached either to labour or birth under water (10).

A documentary film of the maternity unit at Pithiviers, including a birth in the water pool, was made by the BBC and was shown on television in 1982. This powerful and moving film was inspirational and generated widespread interest in the possibility of using water to assist birth. Throughout the 1980s the use of water pools has spread all over the world. The authors' interest in the use of water for labour and birth began in 1982 after meeting Michel Odent. In New Zealand a water birth centre was started by 'The Dolphin Lady', Estelle Myers, and the first water births also occurred in the USA. In 1987 it was estimated that approximately 3,000 babies all over the world had been born in water. As we enter the 1990s the the use of a water pool during labour and birth is rapidly becoming a popular option.

MAMMALIAN INSTINCTS AND REPRODUCTIVE HABITS

As humans we belong to the kingdom of the mammals and, in common with other mammals, we are vertebrate and nourish our young from special mammary glands.

All mammals including man share a similar reproductive system which depends on the interaction of hormones from the mother's pituitary gland and the ovaries producing a phenomenon known as the oestrous or ovarian cycle. However, the reproductive patterns, habits and the length of gestation among mammals varies widely. After birth all mammals are nourished by milk secreted by the mother's mammary glands and the composition of this milk varies to suit the needs of each species.

Social behaviour in mammals varies widely but the dependence of the young mammal on its mother for nourishment is responsible for the close interaction between parent and infant, which generally lasts throughout the primal period until the end of infancy.

Mammals are found all over the world and have an amazing capacity to adapt to varying environmental conditions with a tremendous diversity of form and habits. Every major habitat on earth is inhabited by mammals, both on land and in water. During the past 70,000,000 years mammals have adapted to life on the ground, beneath the ground, in trees and in the air as well as in marine and freshwater habitats. Mammals are remarkable in their ability to acclimatise to environmental extremes by forming new behavioural habits and particular physiological adaptions.

The Dutch biologist Cornelis Naaktegeboren points out the tremendous ability of mammals to adapt their reproductive habits to particular ecological conditions in the struggle for life and preservation of the species (12).

We may ask ourselves whether the attraction amongst modern women to giving birth in water is another example of the mammalian talent for adaption under hostile conditions. When women are overwhelmed by the over-medicalisation of modern techno-obstetrics, they lose their instinctive capacity to give birth. In such conditions humans usually need help to give birth. The worldwide increase in the need for intervention such as induction of labour, caesarian section, forceps delivery and episiotomy, is ample evidence of the failure of the usual maternity unit in a hospital to provide the appropriate conditions to facilitate the birth process.

Naaktegeboren has noted, during his observations of the birthing habits of different species of mammals, that all share a common need to feel safe during labour. When the labouring animal is removed from her safe environment, uterine contractions are usually inhibited. He points out how moving human mothers from home into the unfamiliar surroundings of a modern hospital is stressful and can inhibit a normal labour. He says that suppression of uterine activity is a normal, life-saving response when a labouring animal is threatened by danger. In these circumstances, labour will stop to enable mother and baby to flee in safety. He stresses that in the process of civilization human mothers have not lost these fundamental mechanisms. The diminishing of contractions which is common in mothers when they enter hospital in labour is, he says, an understandable and healthy mammalian response to the unfamiliar environment. While acknowledging the value of modern obstetrics when birth is complicated, difficult or when a problem or emergency arises, many women perceive a hospital environment as hostile, alien or frightening.

The presence of a water pool has a transformative effect in a hospital. When a pool of water is introduced in a quiet and darkened room, the disturbances and distractions which commonly surround the mother in a busy labour ward are reduced. She can regain her connection with her sensuality and the control of her body she needs to give birth. She feels comparatively protected from the intrusion of others. The birth attendants too are calmed and reassured by the presence of water. We can now begin to raise the question of whether the entirely new phenomenon of human mothers giving birth in water is in fact a typically mammalian adaption which we are making in response to the new ecological conditions of modern technological childbirth.

AQUATIC MAMMALS – THE CETACEANS

Perhaps, in introducing water to the birthing room, we are also discovering some deeper instincts which originated millions of years ago in our mammalian history. While most mammals live and give birth on land, for millions of years there have been mammals which give birth in water. The hippopotamus is the only land-based mammal which gives birth in shallow fresh waters.

Whales, dolphins and porpoises come from the mammalian order known as Cetacea (13), and they live and give birth entirely in water. They are primarily marine animals and inhabit the seas of the world as well as some tropical rivers and lakes. They are a very ancient group of mammals, having split off from other species very early in the evolutionary history of Mammalia and returned to live in the oceans millions of years ago. They are completely adapted for aquatic life but are typical mammals in that they carry their young internally until birth. They hold their breath when swimming under water for long periods and breathe through blowholes on the top of their heads when they rise to the surface. They are warm-blooded and give birth in the sea, nursing their young with milk during infancy. Their reproductive habits have many features in common with our own.

Cetaceans usually live in schools, and groups of mothers with young are generally found together near the centre of a school. Studies of bottle-nosed dolphins have shown that the mother-young relationship often persists for several years, with the young returning to its mother in times of stress even when fully grown. Such a group usually has other 'single' females who may act as midwives assisting during birth and also in defence against males.

Cetacea are conceived in an aquatic environment and mating is orgasmic and usually takes place belly to belly like humans. An exception is the humpback whales who have very conspicuous mating behaviour in which they leap right out of the water. Observers report that the male and female swim towards each other in the water at great speed and then mate belly to belly like humans and surface vertically making huge lashing movements with their tails. They rise out of the water completely as they climax and then separate as they dive back into the waves. The length of pregnancy varies from 11–16 months in different species. The 'calves' are well-developed and quite large before they are born. Birth takes place under the water and lasts between 25 minutes and 2 hours. Usually the tail emerges first. After birth, the newborn is nudged to the surface by its mother or by an attendant female, for the first breath. Contact with air stimulates the opening of the blowhole. The umbilical cord snaps off of its own accord close to the umbilicus, the baby begins to swim immediately and within a few hours the fins and flukes harden. Soon after birth the baby cetacea is perfectly adapted to its aquatic environment.

The young will stay close to their mother for weeks, positioning themselves near to the midpoint of her body so they are carried along by the flow of the water alongside her. The nursing span after birth varies but may continue as long as 18 months with dolphins. Feeding takes place from paired mammary glands, with the baby thrusting its snout into a mammary slit, taking the nipple in its tongue to form a tube to receive the milk.

Heathcote Williams describes the birth of a Blue Whale calf in his poetic work *Whale Nation:*

> *Eleven months later*
> *The first sounds a whale calf hears*
> *Is singing.*
> *The mother lifts her newborn calf to the surface*
> *and rolls onto her side,*
> *Expressing her milk into its mouth with*
> *muscles deep inside her breasts:*
> *Twice as rich in protein as human milk*
> *Richer than clotted cream.*

Cetaceans are extraordinary animals which are a source of great fascination to man. While the seas are full of cetaceans (and would be more so were it not for the destructiveness of commercial whalers and fishermen), they are far from overcrowded. Unlike man, they have the capacity to live very harmoniously within their ecosystem.

There are many researchers who believe that the intelligence of Cetacea is equal or even superior to man, especially in their capacity for psychic communication. Whereas the human brain evolved over the past few million years, the cetacean brain dates from 15–20 million years ago. They are certainly capable of very advanced communication systems, have a highly developed acoustic sense and are highly sensitive listeners. They use sonar or sound waves to navigate in the deep seas and can send underwater song cycles from one side of an ocean to another. They have the ability to use sound waves like radar to penetrate the body of other cetaceans, fish or even humans, enabling them to 'see' inside the body and sense emotional fluctuations or physiological changes. Communication at this level is beyond that reached by humans.

Cetacea are very agile in water and capable of very precise formation swimming patterns. They can perform spectacular acrobatic leaps out of the water and enjoy great agility in swimming and riding the waves. They are well-known for their playfulness and the freedom of their sexual expression, and they spend a great deal of time in love play beyond that which is needed for procreation. They have very humane sensibilities and show great tenderness. They will protect each other, assist another animal in trouble or stand by a wounded or sick animal for long periods and mourn and lament their dead. They take great care of their young, shielding and guarding them with their flippers.

Cetaceans have a benign and friendly relationship with man and do not retaliate aggressively, even when provoked. There are many accounts of whales, porpoises and dolphins rescuing drowning humans.

Human communication with dolphins and whales is the subject of much current research. There is a tribe of aborigines on the coast of Northern

Australia who are called the 'Dolphin People'. Their shamans are said to summon the dolphins by whistling and then communicate with them 'mind to mind' (14). There are many who believe that dolphins have much to teach us through their ability to live without aggression and exist in a spirit of true freedom and joy of living.

DOLPHINS AND PREGNANCY

Dolphins are said to be especially fascinated by pregnant mothers and there are some who feel that they can be very helpful to humans during pregnancy and childbirth. Perhaps the assonance of the ancient Greek words for dolphin (delphis) and womb (delphys) is more than a coincidence!

Using inbuilt sonar, dolphins are sensitive to the presence of the baby in the womb of the pregnant mother. Igor Tjarkovsky visits the Black Sea every summer where there are large numbers of dolphins. The pregnant mothers who accompany him are encouraged to get to know the dolphins and spend time swimming with them in the sea during their pregnancy, overcoming their initial fears. Tjarkovsky claims that the dolphins help the mothers and babies to relax. Some of these women were later filmed giving birth in the sea water in the company of dolphin 'midwives'. Besides Tjarkovsky, other people who have swum with dolphins have reported that they seem to have an 'emotion-changing' quality which is said to relax the humans they encounter under water. (15) (16)

Heathcote Williams describes the ability of dolphins to relax humans in his poem *Falling for a Dolphin*. He describes his experience of swimming with a dolphin in the sea and the high frequency vibrations which the dolphin transmits to its underwater companion:

And as the invisible fibres of high frequency
sounds pervade you,
They seem to be slyly skinning you of antique
armouring,
Stressful inconsistencies.
Your grip on the little basket of human manias
you clutch so firmly
Relaxes......

Igor Tjarkovsky has spent many years researching the relationship between mammals and water. He has found that, when trained to do so, even mammals like cats, notorious for their dislike of water, will give birth and nurture their young in an aquatic environment (17). Tjarkovsky believes that man's close affinity with aquatic mammals can be explained by our common origins in water in our mammalian history. He points out that newborn humans can move more easily independently from their mothers in water than on land. Their movements make more sense in an aquatic environment giving them greater agility at an earlier age so that they can swim before they crawl or walk. He claims that a baby's need for oxygen underwater is less since less energy is being used to oppose gravity, and that it is possible for the baby to stay under water for several minutes before coming up for air.

When videos and photographs of Tjarkovsky's water babies swimming under water like little dolphins were first seen in the West they impressed and interested people all over the world. Tjarkovsky's work has some extreme and controversial aspects, but he is to be credited as the pioneer of the use of water for birth and for drawing our attention to our affinity with the aquatic mammals. He has raised many questions which as yet remain open-ended about the benefits and significance of water in the evolution of human life – particularly during the primal period.

Michel Odent, in his book *Water and Sexuality*, suggests that man is by nature an aquatic mammal (18). He shows us how many of our biological features are similar to dolphins and indicate physiological adaption for aquatic life. He points out the erotic power of water and the important role that water plays in human sexuality, including birth.

> For many thousands of years the countless philosophers and scholars who pronounced on human nature did so without seeing that man is first an aquatic primate. The time has come for a radically new version of man.

Odent presents a fascinating argument to explain the power and great attraction of water to humans. Through being more in touch with water he believes we have the possibility to be more in touch with ourselves, our sexual instincts and our basic human nature and to reconcile the gap between instinct and reason. If, as he suggests, water is the missing link with our past, then the attraction to water during labour and giving birth in water can be clearly understood as a vital element in the exciting reconnection modern women are making with their childbearing instincts. Odent's views can be substantiated by writers such as Elaine Morgan, who propose an alternative to Darwin's theory of evolution. In her books *The Aquatic Ape* and *The Descent of Woman*, Elaine Morgan gives a fascinating account of the Aquatic Theory of Evolution as first put forward by Alister Hardy in the 1960s (19). She suggests that Darwinism does not take female physiology or reproductive habits into account. According to her theory our affinity with water goes back millions of years to the Pliocene age, when our ape ancestors lived a semi-aquatic life on the coastline to escape the extreme heat which occurred due to climatic changes. By wading in the sea our ancestors began to walk upright and lost their body hair and developed a layer of subcutaneous fat like other aquatic mammals to protect them from the cooler temperatures of the water. According to her, the earliest evidence of the remains of human woman have been found by archaeologists near to sources of water. There are also now several accounts of modern women who have chosen to give birth in the sea (21).

In the light of all these ideas and the positive experiences of women who have tried it, the use of water during labour and birth is an important new option and cannot be passed over as a mere fad or fashion.

One month before birth an 'aquatic' mother plays in water like a dolphin

2
The Meaning of Water in Our Lives

LIFE BEGINS IN WATER

We live in water for the first nine months of our lives. Deep inside our mother's body we are conceived in the watery fluid of the fallopian tube. A journey by water, which lasts about a week, takes us from the site of conception towards the womb. There we implant in the soft nourishing walls of the uterus and we are surrounded by its fluids and by our mother's blood which sustains us. Our earliest days are spent floating in a vast timeless ocean deep inside her body. During embryonic development, the head region of a human resembles that of a fish at a comparative stage. In the first 8 weeks of life we pass through the evolutionary stages of waterborn existence and retain many of these features later on, while others are adapted or disappear.

In the months to follow, the constant caress of water on our skins gives us our very first sensations. The skin is the first sense organ to develop in utero. It originates from the same part of the embryo as the brain and nerves. Stimulation of its sensitive nerve endings by the warm amniotic fluid gives us the first touch on the surface of our bodies known as 'primal skin feelings'. These sensations help to give us our first primitive sense of 'self', of who we are, of where we begin and end, of our own boundaries and our surroundings.

THE WATER IN OUR BODIES

Water is composed of two elements – each of its molecules is made up of two atoms of hydrogen and one of oxygen. Its shape depends upon the object which contains it and its consistency depends on its temperature, forming ice at its coldest and steam at its hottest. Water is within us and all around us – it is the essential elixir of all life.

Humans are, for the most part, made of water. It is the most important, as well as the most abundant, inorganic substance in our bodies. About 60% of our red blood cells, 75% of our muscle tissue and 92% of our blood plasma is water and even our bones contain water.

Water is a vital ingredient in the working mechanisms of our bodies. The oxygen we inhale and the carbon dioxide we exhale dissolves in the water of our blood and is thus transported between our body cells, the red blood cells and the lungs. Without water none of the chemical reactions which are essential to life could take place. It helps us to digest our food and excrete our waste products. It maintains our body temperature and lubricates our internal organs and joints. In short it is a vital element for our survival.

The water in our cells, connective tissues and blood stream contains many dissolved minerals, mainly sodium and chloride. Thus within every cell there is a minature sea. Hence our tissue fluids and sweat are salty to the taste. Our very essence is an internal ocean.

THE AQUASPHERE

Viewed from outer space it is easy to see that around 70% of the earth's surface is covered by water. From space the earth is seen as a deep blue globe, capped by the white polar ice fields and flecked with wispy patches of soft white cloud beneath which the great continents look like islands. Ninety-seven percent of our planetary water supply is in the great oceans where life began, billions of years ago.

The oceans teem with life, and are rich in minerals and organic substances. Ocean water is the home of the micro-flora, the tiny floating plants in the sea which generate most of the essential oxygen supply of our planet.

Two percent of the planet's water is frozen as ice or snow on the polar ice caps, glaciers and the snow and ice of the high mountain ranges. This water, in ice form, plays the vital role of acting as the planet's temperature moderator. By reflecting the sun's heat the ice assists in cooling the earth.

The water in freshwater lakes, streams and rivers and the ground makes up less than 1% and the rest moves through the atmosphere as rain, fog, mist, cloud and vapour. The water of the oceans and seas is drawn up by evaporation and then falls upon the land as rain in an eternal revivifying cycle.

The primary use of the planet's water is to sustain all living matter, both animal and vegetable and indeed the planet itself. Fresh water is essential for all land-based creatures and, like all life-forms, man cannot live without it.

THE SYMBOLIC MEANING OF WATER

Humans have always lived near or by water – either on the seashore or the river-side. Until our modern age of industrial pollution, the seas, rivers and lakes have been venerated and regarded as sacred since time immemorial. The Ganges in India, for example, is regarded by the Hindus as the sacred mother, and to die beside her is to find union with God. In the Hindu Vedas, water is referred to as 'Matritamah' (the most maternal). Indeed, in cultures all over the world, water, like earth, is symbolic of the Great Mother and is associated with birth, the feminine principle, the universal womb and prima materia.

Water is found throughout nature. It is always in motion and as it moves it reflects the world, changing its colour in the light of the sun or stars. This everflowing element has many transmutations: clear water; spring water; running water; stagnant water; dead water; fresh and salt water; reflecting water; purifying water; deep water; stormy water or calm water. It has a voice and can be silent, murmur gently when tranquil or rage and roar when it is tempestuous. Water has many powers. It has the ability to refresh men and animals and to restore new life to dried out vegetation. It can heal and purify and also has the capacity to destroy.

Water symbolizes the original fountain of life, which precedes all form and all creation. Many myths and legends are based on a concept of there being a primaeval ocean or watery abyss which was the source of all life.

It was called 'Nu' by Ancient Egyptians and 'Apsu' by the Mesopotamians, who regarded it as a symbol of unfathomable impersonal wisdom. There are many examples of life or beauty emerging from water as in the Graeco-Roman tradition when Aphrodite or Venus rose from the water. The Chinese regard water as the abode of the dragon, because all life comes from the waters. In the Hebrew view of creation it is said that, 'the Spirit of God moved on the face of the Waters' and that 'the waters of the Torah' are the life-giving waters of the sacred law. In the Islamic Qoran it is said, 'From the water we made every living thing'. According to Maoris, paradise is under the waters which symbolise primordial perfection.

Water is a life-giving vivifying force. Heavenly rainwater moistens the earth and is also associated with the flowing life forces of our body such as blood, sweat and semen. In this sense, water is equated with movement, moisture and circulation of blood and sap as opposed to the dryness or static condition of death.

Water is also a symbol of fertility. In many ancient or primitive languages the same word is used for water, river or semen, and rainwater is perceived as containing the inseminating power of the sky god. As dew, water symbolises a heavenly blessing on the earth or spiritual refreshment.

In myths, legends and tribal rituals, springs and rivers are the source of holy water with magical powers to enhance fertility. For example, the ancient Egyptians worshipped the fecundity of the Nile as the great symbol of birth, regeneration and fertility symbolised by the God Hapi, who pours water from two pots.

Many religious rituals involve the use of water for purification by sprinkling or immersion. In a baptism, for example, water is used to celebrate and sanctify entry into a new community or life. Immersion in water revives the life force and is used in ritual as a means to spiritual rebirth. In this sense the water signifies a return to the preformal state or to a primordial state of purity with a sense of death and annihilation on the one hand leading through water to rebirth and regeneration.

In Buddhist philosophy, 'crossing the stream' symbolises passing through the world of illusion to enlightenment. Sometimes water in the form of a flood or deluge is the means by which the decadence of an entire population is expiated (i.e. Noah's Flood) after which a new world is created. In dreams the everflowing and transmuting fluid quality of water is often interpreted as a symbol of the collective and personal unconscious and the non-formal or motivating female side of the psyche.

In astrology the water signs, Cancer, Scorpio and Pisces represent the more intuitive, sensitive and feeling qualities of the personality.

Calm, clear water is a symbol of peace and contemplation. Water has been used since ancient times as an oracle for divination. Visions and reflections in water have been used by seers to reveal the past and foresee the future and this is how the modern custom of using crystal balls for fortune telling originated. There is also a transitional quality to water in which its everflowing nature and state of perpetual flux symbolises change or movement. Crossing water often signifies a change from one mode of experience or reality to another. Water can be a means of separation from one side to another. The great-sage's ability to walk on water symbolises transcending the conditions of the phenomenal world. Diving into deep water is a way to explore the mysterious and to search for the secrets of life.

In the Taoist view, water symbolises the strength of weakness and the power of adaption and persistence in its capacity to flow and fill the given space. It represents unity and the fluidity of life as opposed to the separateness and rigidity of death. Water, according to the Taoist view, is the expression of the doctrine of wu-wei – 'giving at the point of resistance', it envelops and passes beyond it, ultimately wearing down even the hardest rock.

Water never rests, neither by day nor
by night. When flowing above, it causes rain
and dew. When flowing below, it forms streams
and rivers. Water is outstanding in doing good.
If a dam is raised against it, it stops.
If way is made for it, it flows along that path.
Hence it is said that it does not struggle
and yet it has no equal in destroying that
which is strong and hard.
Lao Tse
Chochod Louis, *Occultisme et Magic en Extreme-Orient*, Paris, 1945.

THE RITUAL USE OF WATER DURING CHILDBIRTH

Exploring the nature and character of water and reflecting on its symbolic and cultural significance provides us with many insights and clues as to its power to assist women during pregnancy and when giving birth.

The birth of a child follows the breaking of the water and the opening of the womb. When a child is born into a pool, water provides a transition between the inner world of the womb and the outer world of the atmosphere.

For the mother, birth is a rite of passage and a transition from womanhood to motherhood. The pregnancy is left behind and her old identity prior to motherhood changes so that the birth of the baby signifies the birth of a new mother, father and family. The mother's immersion in water during pregnancy, labour and birth has a ritual, as well as practical, value in enhancing her spiritual and psychological transformation. Bathing can be experienced as preparation and purification prior to the celebration of birth.

The birth of a child is a sacred occasion in family life. When a woman labours in an environment in which this is understood and respected, a rare and holy atmosphere can be felt by everyone who is present. The high energy and change of consciousness which occurs during labour is followed by a feeling of euphoria which usually lasts for several weeks after the birth.

Today, many parents and their attendants, all over the world, are recognising that every child can and should be welcomed in a spirit of respect and celebration. We no longer need to hesitate in saying that birth is also a spiritual occasion and in this sense the purifying and sanctifying properties of water are significant.

During the long hours of her labour as her body opens to give birth, a woman experiences a tremendous change of consciousness. At this time she needs to let go of her thinking mind and of the phenomenal world to allow the involuntary and instinctive urges of her body to take over. The qualities of a calm pool of warm water are ideal facilitators of the kind of surrender which is essential during birth.

During pregnancy as well as birth the healing, vivifying, refreshing and health-giving qualities of water can strengthen and nourish both mother and baby and this continues to be helpful throughout infancy. The feminine qualities of water help the mother to access her feminine power and to counteract or dissolve the harsh masculine forces which have dominated childbirth since the invention of obstetric forceps three hundred years ago. Warm water relaxes, comforts and soothes us. Its fluid quality delights the senses and brings us into harmony with our sensuality and sexuality. It offers the woman in labour a way to get in touch with the original freedom of her body and to find the inner unity and peace she needs to nourish and give birth to her child. When a woman carries a child, gives birth to and mothers her baby, she needs to draw on her inner resources for power, energy, strength and endurance. She can be aided in this by the elemental forces of nature. Seen in this perspective we can begin to understand why women who have regained their freedom to give birth are intuitively drawn to water and to the power it has as an ally for childbearing and mothering. This is an era when many of us would like to think that the routine use of obstetric hardware is coming to an end. The feminising and mysterious influence of water in the birth room may indeed, as the Taoists believe, 'have no equal in destroying that which is strong and hard' and in helping mothers and midwives to regain childbirth as women's domain.

3

The Effects of Water Immersion During Labour and Birth

Thousands of women all over the world have found water helpful during labour and birth and their enthusiasm has been shared by their birth attendants. In this chapter we will look at the way immersion in water, or hydrotherapy, affects the mother during labour and birth and how these effects, both physiological and emotional, might influence the birth process. The information available at the present time about the effects of immersion in water during childbirth is based on the empirical experience of mothers and their attendants and some studies. We have found that, when a pool is available, the majority of mothers choose to use it at some time during labour and birth and most of them find it very helpful.

At the Hospital of St. John & St. Elizabeth there are five birthing rooms, each with its own bathroom and two rooms with a specially designed birthing pool large enough to accommodate two adults and to allow for the needs of women in labour. Two-thirds of the mothers use warm water at some time during labour and a quarter give birth in the pool.

The Active Birth Centre produces both portable and permanently installed pools which are in use for home births and in a variety of hospitals in Britain and abroad. They are used in a broad spectrum of settings, by parents, midwives and doctors.

WHAT HAPPENS WHEN THE MOTHER ENTERS THE POOL?

In the 3rd Century BC the Greek inventor and mathematician Archimedes discovered the physical law of buoyancy – known as the Archimedes Principle. This states that any body which is completely or partially submerged in a fluid at rest, is acted upon by an upward or buoyant force. The magnitude of this force is equal to the weight of the volume of fluid which is displaced by the body, when totally or partially immersed. The buoyant force is always opposite in direction to the floating object and will be relative to its weight. The object will, therefore, be supported by the buoyancy of the water.

For example, when a ship is launched it will sink into the ocean until the weight of the water it displaces is equivalent to its own weight. At that depth it will float. If the ship is then loaded with a heavy cargo it will sink deeper, displace more water and the magnitude of the buoyant force will increase proportionately. If the weight of the object is less than the water it displaces, the object will rise, like a block of wood or a cork rises in water.

Fluid pressure increases as water becomes deeper and its weight increases. Buoyancy is caused by this increase in fluid pressure at increasingly greater depth. The pressure on a submerged object, therefore, is greater on the parts more deeply submerged.

When a woman enters a pool of water in labour, the buoyant force exerted on her body will be equal in magnitude to the weight of the volume of water her body has displaced. This upward buoyant force acts in opposition to gravity and will support the mother's body. This results in a feeling of virtual weightlessness and allows the mother respite from the effects of gravity. The buoyant force will be greater the more deeply the mother's body is immersed. Therefore a water pool which allows her to be submerged as deeply as possible is more effective in reducing the effects of gravity than a shallow bathtub or pool.

BUOYANT FORCE

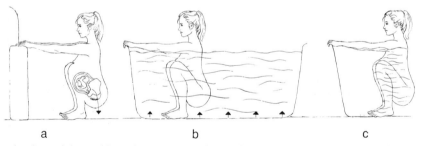

     a   b   c

a) In upright positions the downward force of gravity assists the descent of the baby on land
b) The upward force of buoyancy supports the mother's body weight in water
c) The weight of the water displaced by the mother's body is equivalent to the buoyant force

GRAVITY AND BUOYANCY

Active Birth

Gravity plays a very important role during labour and birth. When a woman uses upright positions such as standing, sitting, kneeling or squatting, her body is in harmony with the downward forces of gravity (see Chapter 5). If, on the other hand, she reclines or sits in the semi-reclining position, gravity pulls in opposition to the angle of the baby's descent through the pelvic canal and the movement of the uterus when it contracts. The following table shows the relationship of body position to gravity and how this might affect the progress of labour and birth.

	Upright Positions (standing/kneeling/squatting etc.)	Reclining Positions (supine position/semi-reclining)
1	Gravity Effective	Opposes Gravity
2	The weight of the baby's body and head exerts pressure on the cervix. Dilation faster.	Less pressure from the baby's head on the cervix – slower dilation.
3	The uterus tilts forward when it contracts. If the mother is upright and leaning forward her uterus contracts without resistance from gravity, resulting in more efficient contractions and less pain.	The uterus works against gravity when it contracts. This results in less efficient contractions and more pain.
4	There is less pressure on the large blood vessels which run along the front of the mother's spine. This results in better blood flow to and from the uterus, an optimal supply of oxygen to the baby and less risk of foetal distress.	The weight of the heavy uterus rests directly on the large blood vessels. This can compromise blood flow so that foetal distress is more likely.
5	There is less pressure on the pelvic ligaments and joints, therefore less pain.	More pressure on pelvic ligaments and joints may result in more pain – especially backache if the baby's head is pressed against the mother's sacrum.
6	In these positions the back wall of the pelvis, formed by the sacrum, is mobile. Its pivotal movement allows the pelvic canal to expand and adjust to the shape of the descending head of the baby.	The mother's weight rests directly on the sacrum. It is then immobile and the result is narrowing of the pelvic canal and loss of flexibility.
7	During bearing down the upright position, especially squatting, enables the uterus to exert the maximum force to help the birth.	The bearing down force is minimized if the mother is horizontal. This prolongs the second stage of labour.

	Upright Positions (standing/kneeling/squatting etc.)	Reclining Positions (supine position/semi-reclining)
8	The baby's direction of descent in these positions is down and out in harmony with gravity. Rotation, descent of the head and expulsion will be easiest with the pelvic birth canal vertical.	The mother's birth canal is horizontal. The baby's descent is at 90 degrees to gravity. Rotation and descent of the head will be less efficient and expulsion is likely to be more difficult.
9	In the final contractions of the second stage the perineal tissues can stretch and expand more easily. The pressure is evenly distributed over the entire vaginal outlet as the baby's head emerges. This reduces the likelihood of tearing.	The baby's head exerts pressure towards the back of the vaginal outlet or the perineum. This increases the risk of injury to the perineal and vaginal tissues and the underlying pelvic floor muscles.
10	The mother's coccyx is free and mobile and moves to widen the pelvic outlet.	As the mother's weight is resting directly on it, the coccyx is immobilized so that the pelvic outlet is narrowed and there is more risk of injury to the coccyx during the birth.

Conclusions: A woman is not designed to give birth lying down. While the reclining positions are more convenient for the attendants, they are least effective for mother and baby. The birth will be more efficient, easier, safer and faster if the mother uses gravity-effective positions to give birth to her baby (1).

These facts have been confirmed by numerous studies (2). The most powerful confirmation comes from women themselves, who naturally move and position their bodies in harmony with gravity when they have the freedom to follow their instincts. Since time immemorial, women all over the world have naturally found upright positions most comfortable and effective for labour and birth. It is only in the last 300 years, since the invention of forceps heralded the birth of modern obstetrics, that the reclining position became fashionable and we lost the help of gravity during childbirth. It is now widely understood that if the mother's body position opposes gravity, birth is more likely to be difficult, complications will increase and interventions will be more necessary.

Buoyancy
When a pregnant woman in labour enters a pool of water the effects of gravity on her body are very much reduced by the counter pressure of the water, but, unlike the reclining positions, there is no opposition to gravity. The resulting

near weightlessness allows the mother's body to be supported by the water. It becomes much easier for her to move and adopt any position she chooses. This in itself will assist her to use her body instinctively, by moving to release tightness or tension and ease the pain she experiences as her cervix dilates. The buoyancy of the water allows her to relax and to spend less energy in supporting her weight, giving her more energy to cope with the contractions and greater relaxation in the intervals between them. She can easily adopt positions which open her pelvis and move her body to assist the descent of her baby through the birth canal.

Contractions can sometimes slow down and become less efficient when the mother enters the pool. When this happens it is best to leave the pool and make the most of the help of gravity. Sometimes maximal pressure from the baby's head on the dilating cervix is essential and being underwater is not helpful. At the end of labour, in the second stage, the force of the expulsive reflex may sometimes be reduced in water and it becomes more practical to use a supported squat position on land. A water pool is most helpful when the woman and her attendants understand how to make the best use of gravity.

WHAT CAUSES PAIN IN LABOUR?

Pain in labour is caused by a complex combination of physical and psychological factors. Although the precise physiology is not yet understood, the following factors are bound to influence the mother's perception of pain in labour:

- The intensity and quality of uterine contractions. Pain arises from the muscle fibres and is maximal at the height of a contraction as the nerve fibres in the uterus are stimulated by the muscle activity. Pain also arises from the stretching of the dilating cervix and lower segment of the uterus during contractions in labour.
- The size, shape and position of the baby relative to the mother's pelvis.
- The relationship between the force of gravity, uterine contractions and the mother's posture will influence the degree of pain. The most comfortable positions are usually the most mechanically advantagous, enhancing labour while reducing pain.
- Stretching of the pelvic ligaments, soft tissues and joints and stimulates the nerves.
- In the second stage, pain is due to stretching of tissues in the vagina, the vulva or the perineum, and to the widening of the pelvic joints.
- Resistance or inhibition due to psychological factors such as fear, anxiety or tension or environmental stress may be key factors in the perception of pain during labour. When the mother's hormonal and physiological environment is upset, muscular tension increases, the natural opiates secreted by her body known as endorphins are reduced and pain increases (3). (See page 33)

The degree of pain which a woman experiences in labour and her ability to tolerate it depends upon the complex interplay of all of the above and other factors. Immersion in water can influence all these factors to a considerable degree.

HOW PAIN PERCEPTION ALTERS IN WATER

To understand how water can affect the perception of pain, it is useful to look at the way painful impulses are transmitted. We have seen how, in labour and during birth, pain may arise from the uterus, cervix, pelvic joints and ligaments, the vagina, vulva and perineum. Nerve fibres carry the impulses from pain receptors at the site of the painful stimulus to the dorsal horn of the spinal cord. From there they are transmitted to the cerebral cortex in the brain.

'The Gate Control Theory'

In the 1970s Wall and Melzack put forward this theory to explain pain modification (4).

The dorsal horn extends the entire length of the spinal cord. Impulses from nerves all over the body arising from stimuli such as pain, touch or temperature

THE GATE THEORY OF PAIN

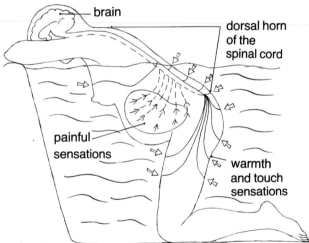

All sensations converge in the dorsal horn of the spinal cord. Pain sensations are modified or partially 'gated out' by competing sensations of warmth and touch on the mother's skin when she is immersed in water during labour.

a) Painful sensations arising from the uterus and pelvis travel along pain receptor nerves to the spinal cord and then to the brain.

b) The dorsal horn of the spinal cord runs along its entire length.

c) Touch and warmth sensations on the mother's skin from the water travel along specific receptor nerves to the brain via the dorsal horn.

converge in the dorsal horn and are transmitted to the brain.

Some impulses reaching the dorsal horn excite pain transmission and others inhibit it. The amount of pain perceived will depend on the balance of impulses. There are many different nerve fibres in the dorsal horn which transmit stimuli at different speeds. Pain impulses are transmitted more slowly than, say, touch and pressure. As these sensations reach the dorsal horn faster than the pain impulses, it is thought that they have the effect of dampening the transmission of the pain impulse from the level of the spinal cord before they reach the brain. In this sense they close the 'gate' to pain sensations. In other words, the nerve endings in the skin which respond to sensations of warmth and touch are stimulated by the feeling of the water on the mother's whole body. These, and the muscles of the hair follicles relaxing, releasing pleasant sensations from the periphery, are transmitted to the dorsal column of the spine along with the pain sensations and serve to inhibit or reduce the transmission of some of the painful impulses. In even simpler terms the pleasant sensations reach the brain faster and help to reduce awareness of the painful ones. Water immersion stimulates touch and temperature fibres throughout the body, thereby creating a background of a large number of pleasurable sensations. The pain sensations are superimposed on this background and have to compete for access to the spinal cord and brain. Pain is partially or completely 'gated out'.

Pain Relieving Hormones

The endocrine system of mother and baby releases hormones or chemical messengers throughout pregnancy, birth, and breast feeding. The physiology of the endocrine system during birth is complex. Hormones trigger off the sequence of involuntary responses which affect the contractile power of the uterus, initiate labour, and end after the birth with the expulsion of the placenta and the start of breastfeeding. Oxytocin is one of the hormones secreted by the pituitary gland which stimulate the uterus to contract and breastmilk to eject.

One system of hormones which have an important role to play in labour are the endorphins. These act as natural painkillers and may also have an oxytocic effect (i.e. stimulate contractions). Our bodies are capable of increasing the production of endorphins in labour as a physiological response to the increasing level of pain. They are released by the stem of the brain and in the dorsal horn. They then bind themselves to special opiate receptors in the nerve endings and inhibit or block the transmission of painful impulses in the spinal cord and brain. At the end of labour endorphin secretion is reduced and the mother's body is thought to secrete the adrenalin type hormones (catecholamines) which stimulate the expulsive contractions of the second stage (5). If, however, catecholamine secretion occurs earlier on in labour due to anxiety, disturbance or stress, these hormones would inhibit uterine contractions and increase pain (3). We can conclude that water works in two ways to influence pain. The combination of endorphins blocking pain fibres with other sensations from the mother's skin 'closing the gate', will work together to reduce the pain of labour. The combination of water and privacy is intensely relaxing and this makes the optimal psychological and physiological environment for minimising pain.

We can, therefore, assume that immersion in warm water in labour activates the part of the brain which is responsible for involuntary activities such as digestion, excretion and sexual orgasm, as well as uterine contractions during labour and birth. This helps the mother to let go of her rational thinking mind and surrender to the instinctive 'primitive' part of her consciousness so that her body can take over, and she can give birth more easily. A water pool can be one of the most effective ways to assist the mother in labour to be free from inhibitions and let go to her instinctive impulses.

CONCLUSIONS
A number of common physical and emotional benefits have been noted by women and their attendants when a water pool is used for labour and birth. These are summarised below, and explained in greater detail in chapter 5.

Greater Comfort and Mobility
Weightlessness induced by the buoyancy of the water reduces opposition to gravity. Under water, the mother has greater ease and freedom to move spontaneously and to change her position. She can more easily assist the descent of her baby and make the most of the expandability of her pelvis. This is especially beneficial to women who are overweight or carrying a large baby, who may otherwise find it difficult to move or change position.

Reduction of Abdominal Pressure
The reduction of abdominal pressure caused by buoyancy promotes more efficient uterine contractions and better blood circulation. This results in better oxygenation to the uterine muscles, hence less pain for the mother and more oxygen for the baby – so less risk of foetal distress (6).

Conservation of Energy
The water reduces opposition to gravity and supports the mother's body weight so that her energy can be used to cope with the contractions.

Pain Relief
Women respond to pain in different ways and water does not provide complete pain relief. However, it usually minimises it to a level where other methods of pain relief are not needed (6, 7, & 8).

The following factors influence pain in water:
- Greater privacy
- Greater mobility
- Weightlessness

- Reduction of abdominal pressure
- Warmth and tactile stimulation
- Hormone secretion
- Relaxation

Facilitating a dysfunctional labour
Water immersion can sometimes be a way to stimulate dilation of the cervix when the mother has difficulty progressing into the active stage of labour (beyond 5 cms) and to reduce the need for drugs to stimulate labour. While it is not always the case, getting into the pool may result in dramatic and rapid progress to full dilation within an hour or two and is usually worth a try (10, 11).

Fall in Blood Pressure
There is a lowering of arterial blood pressure when a woman is immersed in water in labour. When high blood pressure is caused by anxiety, immersion in water may help to bring it down. However, this should not be relied upon in cases where high blood pressure is due to pre-eclampsia (12, 13).

Change of Consciousness
A rapid fall in levels of anxiety soon after the mother enters the water has been observed by most people using water pools. Women who were previously distressed, often become much more relaxed or even sleepy and indifferent to what is going on around them. It then becomes possible to let go to the change of consciousness that occurs in labour. Isolation in water can help to facilitate the mother's withdrawal into herself as labour strengthens.

Breathing
The moist atmosphere in the pool room makes it easier to breathe and this can be especially helpful to women with asthmatic tendencies.

Facilitating the Second Stage
In a water pool, mothers are noticeably less inhibited. In addition there is a very low incidence of injury to the soft tissues of the vagina, vulva and perineum due to the softening effects of the warm water.

These factors usually make the final stages of the birth easier and less traumatic for the mother and baby, provided there is no good reason for the mother to leave the pool and use the help of gravity in the second stage (see page 111).

Sometimes the way that water works is mysterious. As Odent says:

> We have found, for example, that the mere sight of water and the sound of it filling the pool are sometimes sufficient stimuli to release inhibitions so that a birth may occur before the pool is full (14).

Facilitating the Third Stage

After the birth the baby is brought to the surface gently and held in the mother's arms, usually with its body still immersed and its face and head out of the water. Water can provide ideal conditions for the first contact between the parents and the newborn baby and a physiological third stage. The brief transition through water softens the first impact of gravity, the atmosphere, light and sound for the baby so that birth is gentler through the familiar watery medium.

While having considerable benefits to mother and baby as we have seen, the use of water during labour and birth seems to have no harmful side-effects when sensibly used for normal labour. Most of the anxieties about any potential adverse effects centre around the issue of safety and these are dealt with in chapter 7.

There is no greater incidence of infection, perineal injury is less common and most tears that do occur are first degree. Remarkably few babies are born compromised and a very small percentage need further care after birth. However, it is important that the parents' expectations should be realistic and that waterbirth should not become a new dogma resulting in the parents approaching their birth with fixed expectations of having a waterbirth. This is perhaps the greatest risk involved in the use of water for birth (see chapter 5).

The use of a waterpool does not provide total pain relief like an epidural, and it will not always induce contractions as efficiently as an oxytocin drip. There are some instances in which the use of such obstetric practises are bound to be necessary and appropriate. In these cases the need generally outweighs the risks and the result is usually successful. The simple provision and sensible use of the safe and harmless facility of a pool of water can certainly help a large number of women to avoid the need for interventions and the potentially harmful side effects which they entail.

Michel Odent concludes:

> The use of warm water during labour requires further research, but we hope that other experience would confirm that immersion in warm water is an efficient, easy and economical way to reduce the use of drugs and the rate of intervention in parturition (15).

Since 1983, when Odent wrote this article, thousands of experiences including our own have confirmed his observations. The Health Committee Report on Maternity Services for the House of Commons has stated

> We recommend that all hospitals make it their policy to make full provision whenever possible for women to chose the position they prefer for labour and birth, *with the option of a birthing pool where this is practicable* (16).

In Great Britain we can now reasonably expect a water pool to become available as one of a range of options available to every woman in labour in the coming years.

4

Using Water in Pregnancy

There are many ways in which water can be used to enhance your pregnancy.

Having more contact with water at this time can benefit you and your partner as well as your baby tremendously and prepare the way for making the most of water during labour, birth and in the post-natal months.

In this chapter suggestions are made for bathing in the home. These include using essential aromatherapy oils for their pleasurable and therapeutic effects.

Meditation in water can help you to calm your mind and to get more deeply in touch with your feelings in preparation for parenthood, while enhancing communication with your baby before birth. There is a section on learning to use the power of water for relaxation, visualisation and meditation, so that you can use your own bathroom every day as a restorative spa and health-giving retreat.

There is also a programme of water exercises which can be done in a swimming pool throughout your pregnancy and continued post-natally.

BATHING

For many people, bathing is one of the most pleasurable personal rituals of the day. In pregnancy, luxuriating in a tub of warm water is a wonderful way to restore your energy, soothe away tensions and give yourself some respite from the extra weight you are carrying.

The bathroom is a sanctuary within your home where you can relax in privacy and peace. You can enhance the experience with a few simple additions such as curtains or blinds to reduce intensive lighting during the day and an inflatable waterproof pillow for your head. Candles in the evening will transform the atmosphere. You might like to introduce a few plants, and a portable cassette player is useful if you enjoy listening to soothing music in the bath (make sure you position it at a safe distance from the water). Bathing softens and cleanses your skin and relaxes your muscles. It stimulates your circulation, improves sleep and refreshes body and soul. It also provides you with a wonderful opportunity to practise some deep relaxation and meditation and to be more aware of your inner connection with your baby.

Aromatic Baths

The addition of essential oils to the water is a therapeutic way of relaxing, reviving, restoring and healing yourself while bathing. Aromatherapy is a natural healing tradition in which essential plant oils are used in combination with massage, bathing or inhalations. The 'essence' of the tree, plant or flower is extracted by a process of distillation producing a volatile oil which contains the concentrated life force and properties of the plant.

Essential oils enter your bloodstream through your skin and lungs. When added to the bath water they permeate the skin, moisturising it and stimulating the production of new cells. At the same time the aromatic fragrances are inhaled. The olfactory receptors in the nose transmit the odours to the part of the brain known as the limbic system. This connects with other parts of the brain which affect many of our vital body functions including the nervous and reproductive systems and the endocrine system which regulates the release of hormones in our bodies. Essential oils can have remarkably powerful and beneficial effects both physically and emotionally. They can help to soothe and relax, relieve tension and depression, stimulate energy flow, enhance sleep, attack bacteria, stimulate cell production, aid digestion, reduce congestion, improve circulation of blood and lymph and stimulate sexual response.

Make sure that you never use essential oils undiluted. They are very concentrated and should be used with great care, especially during pregnancy when you are particularly sensitive and the effects of the oils will also be reaching your baby. The stronger essences such as rosemary, thyme, basil, common sage, oreganum, wintergreen, tea tree, clove, hyssop, myrrh, cinnamon, bark and pennyroyal should be avoided during pregnancy.

There are hundreds of essential oils to choose from and it is best during pregnancy and postnatally to use a small selection of essences which are gentle in their effects. The essences recommended in this chapter can safely be used in the home at this time. For treatment of any health problem, however, you should consult a trained holistic aromatherapist.

When buying your oils make sure they are pure and natural and obtained from a reputable supplier (see useful addresses). Prices vary and some essential oils can be expensive but should last a long time as you only need a few drops at a time. The essential oils listed below are most suitable for use in pregnancy and after birth.

Lavender
This gentle floral essence is especially useful during the childbearing years. It is soothing and calming, antiseptic and restorative. It stimulates the immune system, promotes cell growth and can be used to treat wounds and burns. Lavender can be used for babies and is helpful for relieving pain in labour (you can add a few drops to the bath or pool water).

Rose
Beautifully fragrant, rose oil is uplifting and anti-bacterial. It regulates the

female sex organs, nourishes the skin and is an anti-depressant sedative and tonic. It benefits the uterus by helping to tonify and regulate uterine activity. It is useful for depression and low libido, nausea, headaches and insomnia both before and after birth and can be used for babies.

Chamomile
This plant has remarkable healing and anti-bacterial powers and is prized for its medicinal properties. It is calming and soothing and is helpful in the treatment of insomnia, nervous tension, digestive problems and skin disorders. One of the best essences to use for babies and baby care products.

Jasmin
An exquisitely aromatic oil, jasmin is known as the king of oils. It has a warm softening effect on the nerves and tendons and is relaxing, soothing and anti-depressant. Its pain relieving properties are useful during labour. Add to the bath or a base oil and massage into your lower back three weeks before your due date.

Rose Geranium
This has a rosy aroma and is a relaxant and tonic. It stimulates the hormonal system and the circulation, is relaxing and beneficial to the skin.

Ylang Ylang
Exotic and fragrant, the oil from these flowers regulates blood pressure and is a sedative, antiseptic and aphrodisiac.

Bergamot
This oil has a calming and anti-depressant effect.

Lemon Grass
Acts directly on the endocrine system and is emotionally strengthening and refreshing.

Lemon, Mandarin, Neroli and Tangerine
These are all members of the citrus family and have a tonic, mildly stimulating and refreshing effect. Tangerine and lemon contain vitamin C and are useful to nourish the skin in pregnancy. Neroli stimulates new cell growth and is helpful in preventing or treating stretch marks.

Peppermint
Stimulant, digestive and cooling. May help headaches or indigestion and makes a very cooling bath in hot weather in pregnancy. Do not use if you are taking homeopathics as peppermint antidotes some remedies.

How to use essential oils in the bath
After you have run your bath, add a total of 4-6 drops of essential oil to the
water and distribute with your hand. The oils are highly volatile so to get the
best effect add them in at the last moment before you enter the water.

Start with one oil at a time and then experiment with combinations of two or
three depending on the desired effects.

Here are some ideas
Relaxing and refreshing – lavender and bergamot
Sleep inducing, sedative – chamomile on its own or ylang-ylang and bergamot
Strengthening and stimulating – lemon grass and lavender
Antidepressant, uplifting, soothing – rose and jasmin
Decongestant – lemon and lavender
Aphrodisiac – ylang ylang
Anti-stretch mark – lavender and neroli
Cooling – peppermint
Relieving aches and pains – chamomile and lavender or geranium

Underwater massage
Massage in water is both delightful and therapeutic. While you are in the bath
you can massage your breasts by gently making smooth stroking movements
from the outer edges towards the nipples (like the spokes of a wheel). Go right
around the circumference of the breast so that each part of the 'circle' is
massaged.

Then massage your upper chest between the breasts and the collar bone
starting from the centre and working outwards towards your shoulders. You
can also massage your belly by gently making smooth circular movements
under the water so that, as you stroke, you are sensitive to the presence of your
baby. Massaging your arms, legs and feet is also beneficial. If a friend or
partner can massage your neck and shoulders and down your spine in the bath,
this can benefit you enormously and stimulate the entire nervous system.

After bath massage
You can make up an aromatic massage oil for after the bath using the same
essences as you used in the water by adding 6 drops of essential oil to 4ozs of a
base oil such as sweet almond oil, grapeseed or wheatgerm. The latter is a very
rich nourishing oil ideal for the skin in pregnancy. If you find it too sticky you
can mix it with almond oil. Alternatively you can buy a ready prepared
aromatherapy oil for pregnancy (see useful addresses). Rose or chamomile
essence in a light base makes a lovely baby massage oil. It is helpful to read a
book on simple massage techniques for pregnancy, after birth and baby
massage (see recommended reading and page 147).

THE MEDITATIVE POWER OF WATER

It is a natural impulse for most people to use water for relaxation and many of us retire to the bath to unwind, solve our problems, daydream or think creatively. Here we can be alone, let the body go and the mind wander and enjoy the sensual pleasure of the warm water. We can share the experience with our sexual partner or children or we can make the most of the opportunity to enjoy some solitude. The time you spend bathing can also be used creatively to deepen your ability to relax and calm your mind through meditation. Practised regularly this will have profound benefits in pregnancy and will also prepare you wonderfully for the change of consciousness that occurs during labour. After the birth you can continue to calm, restore and energise yourself and your baby with the healing effects of bathing (see chapter 6).

Preparing for Relaxation and Meditation in the Bath
Choose a time of day when you will be undisturbed and are free to relax for up to an hour, whether in the morning, afternoon or before going to bed. Prepare for the bath so that you can immerse yourself completely in the experience. Try to fill the bath if possible so that your belly is covered by the water. This will allow you to make the most of the feeling of weightlessness caused by the buoyancy of the water. You may need to boil up one or two additional kettles of hot water to fill the bath up to the top. Make sure that the water temperature is comfortable. It should be warm and not too hot. Adjust the lighting, add any essential oils and put on a tape of quiet meditative music if you want to. Enter the water slowly and allow yourself to float comfortably. If you like, wet your hair and immerse your head under the water for a few moments (do not use any essential oils other than chamomile if you are putting your head under water as they might irritate your eyes). Wax earplugs are not necessary but may be used if you prefer, or if you are not used to putting your head under water. They can be obtained from a pharmacy. This is a very useful exercise for overcoming any fears of water. When you get used to putting your head under the water, try blowing bubbles or making sounds underwater before you come up to inhale. Try opening your eyes when your head is under the water so that you realise you can see through water. This will be especially useful when you are teaching your baby to swim (see page 152). In the section that follows a few meditations are suggested which you may enjoy doing in the bath. Your partner may also like to try them. Work with one meditation for a few weeks before trying another to give it time to deepen. Before you start you can prepare for the experience by doing the following relaxing visualisation.

Relaxing Water Visualisation
Allow yourself to sink down into the bath and experience the feeling of buoyancy and weightlessness in the water. Close your eyes and let your breathing flow comfortably. When you are ready, use your imagination to visualise yourself stepping onto a beautiful beach on a perfectly warm

summer's day. The beach has soft white sand and is surrounded by tall palm trees and lush green vegetation. The leaves are stirring softly in a gentle breeze and you can hear the sound of the waves lapping gently on the shore. Imagine yourself lying down on your back in the soft sand at the waters edge so that the waves break gently over your lower body. Feel the warmth of the sun and the soft carress of the water and the air on your skin. Allow yourself to relax completely as you look up and see the blueness of the sky with a few wisps of pure white fluffy clouds moving slowly across your view. Now imagine closing your eyes. Feel your body sinking down slowly into the softness of the water, supported and caressed by the waves. Breathe deeply and feel that you are getting lighter and lighter until it feels as if your body is floating, completely supported on the water's surface, like a baby in a cradle. Have a feeling of perfect harmony with the natural world around you as if you are resting in the lap of mother earth.

You are now ready to begin the meditation.

Meditation on the Breath

Place your hands gently on your lower belly over your womb. In Chinese medicine this is known as the 'Tantien' or centre of energy.

Keep your eyes closed and breathe slowly in and out through your nose. Don't try to alter the breath in any way, just concentrate on observing it. When you exhale you will notice your belly moving downwards as the air is expelled from your lungs, so that the air seems to empty from your centre. At the end of

the out breath there is a pause, or an empty, still space. When the breath has reached the bottom of the still space, wait and allow the in-breath to come in gradually by itself, like a gift. As the breath comes in, the centre or 'Tantien' expands and becomes full. Then there is a pause at the top of the breath, until the next exhalation begins slowly. Continue like this, focusing your awareness on the flow of the breath. When thoughts arise, acknowledge them and then, when you are ready, return your awareness to your breathing. It may take weeks or even months to be able to sustain your concentration, so don't be despondent if you find yourself easily distracted at first. With practice, your concentration will improve and your meditation will deepen. This will be very useful during labour when you need to let go of thinking and be in your body and at many other times in your life.

Seeing Yourself and Your Baby
The purpose of this deeply relaxing meditation is to come into contact with and to relax every part of your body in turn as you focus your awareness from top to toe and from front to back. While you are pregnant, the meditation can also be used for becoming aware of every part of your womb and also of the placenta and your baby.

Relax in the water with your eyes closed. Begin wherever you like in your body, for example you may begin at the crown or top of your head, where the soft spot of a baby would be. Breathe gently, letting the breath come in and out on its own as you focus your attention on that spot and consciously release any tension. Now move very gently towards your left ear. Focus on the shape of your ear, the warmth and the sensations in your ear and let go of any tension in your ear. Now continue like this all the way down your body including your face, the back of your head, the outside and inside of your throat, the outside and inside of your chest, the outside and inside of your abdomen, the outside and inside of your pelvis and your legs, and so on all the way down to your toes. It does not matter whether you start at the top of your head or whether you start in your abdomen or your fingers, as long as you 'brush down' and release the energy throughout your body as you breathe. Some people find it useful to imagine a spot of light, soft and beautiful, moving slowly over the body from head to toe.

When you have gone through your whole body, focus on your baby and use your imagination to do the same thing, from head to toe, front to back, inside and outside as she floats in the nourishing waters of your womb.

When you first begin you may want to make quick jumps, for example top of your head, your ears, front of your face, back of your head etc; whereas later on, when you become more used to this, you may want to go in much smaller, finer steps. This meditation can be made to last anything from five minutes to an hour or more.

Calming the mind
Most of us find that, when we begin to meditate, our minds are full of thoughts

and it can be difficult to let go of thinking.

Over time this meditation may help you to quieten your mind and experience the blissful peace that is to be found when the 'internal dialogue' we have in our heads becomes quiet. It is done in two parts.

1   Relax in the water and breathe deeply and comfortably. For the next five or ten minutes, consciously observe your thoughts as they come up in your mind. Acknowledge them and watch them, but try not to follow, stop or alter them in any way – just remain conscious of the thoughts and watch them come and go. Continue doing this daily for a period of 14 days and then progress to the second part.

2   When you are relaxed and observing your thoughts, try to 'freeze' the thought and keep looking at it as long as you can. Stay alert and conscious, and when your next thought arises do the same thing. Continue like this, 'freezing' the thoughts as they arise. With some practice you will notice the thoughts becoming less frequent and the calm peaceful spaces inbetween will occur more often as your mind becomes quieter and more tranquil.

When you have learnt to access the meditative powers of your mind it will help you to feel calm and centred and to experience inner harmony and equilibrium. Meditation can be particularly useful if you are afraid or anxious about the birth, or about becoming a mother. The ability to calm yourself, even for a few minutes each day, is an important step towards enjoying and accepting this new phase of your life. Meditation can, of course, be practised on land as well as in water.

EMOTIONS IN PREGNANCY

Having a baby is an experience which is certain to enrich and change your life profoundly. From the very beginning your feelings are bound to be more turbulent. Like water, emotions flow, and in pregnancy they are sometimes especially intense.

Spending time relaxing and meditating in water will encourage your feelings to surface more easily, allowing you to release them gently and to find a sense of calm and equilibrium, even in the face of great excitement, difficulty or conflict. Water is a feminine element which can help you to let go of your rational thinking mind and allow your intuitive, motherly instincts to blossom and develop. Finding the ability to accept and flow with your feelings as they arise is the key to a successful passage from woman to mother. After all, you are going through the important transition, or 'rite of passage', from adult to parent – one of the most significant in the life cycle of any human being.

Coming to terms with the dramatic emotional and physical changes you are going through within your self and your relationships and coping with the new responsibilities and changes to your lifestyle is a fundamental part of the exciting challenge of having a baby. Pregnancy has a way of unearthing a whole range of emotions such as deep-seated anxiety, anger and fear as well as excitement and joyful anticipation.

Most women are amazed at the power and flood of new emotions which surge through them in pregnancy. You may well find that anxieties and fears, or old hurts or guilts from childhood which you had felt you had already dealt with and were long gone, may emerge and come to the surface. This is a time to re-explore such issues or memories from your early life, to come to terms with deep, blocked or suppressed feelings and try to resolve any conflicts in the present. Having a baby can be an incredibly healing and clearing experience which can open new doors and help you to let go of what lies behind you if you are willing to let it happen.

Facing your Fears
Many women encounter intense fears of what lies ahead during pregnancy and this is to be expected when you are about to go through an experience as deep and powerful and even dangerous as birth. Acknowledging the fear is the first and possibly the most important step in accepting pregnancy and the birth that follows. For some men and women this is a very easy natural step along the path to parenthood, whereas for others the fear is so intricately interwoven in their previous experience that it becomes difficult to separate the present from the past. If this is your experience then it is very important to examine and express these feelings during pregnancy, either on your own or with your family and friends or even with the aid of professional help and counselling.

Pregnancy is a time when most women are very open to change. Feelings are more accessible and can be released more easily. Confusion can be easier to sort out than at any other time in your adult life.

You may have specific fears of water, arising from your past, or a lack of experience of water in your childhood. This can result in conflict with the desire to use water during labour and birth. In particular there may be a fear of drowning. It is important to access these feelings during pregnancy so that you can release them and arrive at a feeling of acceptance prior to the onset of labour. This will prevent you conveying your fears of water to your baby after the birth (see page 146).

You may be concerned that getting in touch with so called 'negative' or suppressed feelings in pregnancy could harm your developing baby. This is unlikely since they are part of your reality already and acknowledging, coming to terms with and releasing them will give you a new freedom in which to accept and welcome your baby.

The Father's Feelings
Men differ in the degree to which they want to be involved in their partner's pregnancy, labour and birth. Some enjoy sharing the events of pregnancy and birth and taking an active role in parenting the baby, while others prefer to be supportive in other ways. Some men may have difficulty in coping with the responsibilities and challenges of becoming a father and it is important to recognise that the baby's father is also pregnant!

Fathers may have very definite ideas about the way in which their children should be born, nourished and raised. These are issues which need to be discussed during pregnancy so that you are united and open to responding appropriately to your baby's needs at the time. As parents it is vital to be able to communicate openly with each other and to make the time to both talk and listen.

Some fathers may have experienced difficulties when they themselves were born or may have been acquainted with women, friends, or family who have experienced a complication of labour and birth. If this has happened, anxieties and fears may surface during the pregnancy and/or during the birth itself, and may affect the mother's ability to relax.

While not generally recognised, it is equally important for fathers to prepare emotionally for birth and parenthood (see chapter 5).

Your Baby in Pregnancy

Babies develop emotionally as well as physically during the months they spend in the womb. From early on, they are exquisitively sensitive to the emotional field around them. While you are pregnant you will have many clues as to your child's developing personality in terms of periods of wakefulness and sleep and the way your baby moves. Your baby's mental capacities are developing in the womb and there are periods of rapid eye movement (REM) sleep which is associated with dreaming. In late pregnancy up to 80% of the time your baby sleeps is spent dreaming, whereas in later life dream sleep periods drop progressively. On a psychological and psychic level there is already a deep inner connection between you. Your baby can identify your voice and can also recognise different sounds and music heard in the womb after birth. From the start your baby is an individual with his or her own rhythms, patterns, likes and dislikes. The ebb and flow of your inner communication with your baby is an important part of your pregnancy, preparing you for your relationship after the birth. The daily rhythms, developed in the womb before birth, continue into the newborn period. You will not be surprised to discover that you know your baby and your baby knows you from the time you share together during pregnancy.

The 'bonding' that occurs after the birth has its roots in this early communication which occurs on a multitude of levels and begins soon after conception, becoming more intricate as the baby develops.

Some of the baby's earliest perceptions originate from the stimulation of the amniotic fluid on the sensitive nerve endings in the skin (see page 22). Not surprisingly, in adult life, many of us feel soothed and calmed by immersion in warm water, as if we return each time we bath to the original safe harbour of the womb.

Inside the womb your baby hears many sounds (see baby meditation on page 54), sleeps, dreams and responds to the movements and rhythms of your body. The chemical messages of the hormones crossing from your bloodstream, and your heart beating, affect your baby so that he is aware of your feelings and moods. Your baby also hears the sounds of the movement of food through your digestive system and receives nutrients from the food you eat through your bloodstream. He practises breathing and sucking, swallowing, hiccoughing and urinating into the amniotic fluid, thus playing an active role in maintaining the consistency of the fluid. The baby tones and exercises his body muscles by moving his head, wriggling, rolling over, punching and kicking in the womb.

In late pregnancy, the baby's body fills the uterus and the skin is close to the uterine wall as the volume of amniotic fluid decreases. At this stage the baby can feel your hands as you stroke and massage him and is also massaged by the contractions of your uterus which become increasingly frequent and powerful as birth approaches. Underwater massage in the bath or pool is an enjoyable way to communicate with your baby (see page 40), and is deepened by meditation on the presence of your child.

WATER EXERCISES

Exercising in water is an exciting and joyful experience that can transform the way you feel and introduce you to a new way of living healthily. This programme of gentle water exercise can be used throughout your pregnancy, will aid your recovery after birth and help you to stay energised in the post-natal months.

Regular exercise is essential for your health and vitality at all times, but especially when you are pregnant or nursing a baby. At this time, you are responsible not only for your own health, but for the physical and emotional

Swimming in pregnancy is an ideal way to enhance health and improve fitness

nurturing of your child. Everything you do influences her development from the very beginning. In pregnancy, water can help you to feel energetic and have a positive attitude towards your body, and your baby. When, like your baby, you are in water yourself, it enhances your sense of connection with your child. Babies learn from their mothers throughout pregnancy. The time you spend bathing will already be familiarising your baby with water and encouraging her natural instincts and reflexes to swim. It will also help you to direct your mental energy towards your baby, increasing your awareness of the presence inside you.

If you want to have a water birth or use water during your labour, playing and exercising in water is ideal preparation. The more time you spend in water the better.

It is also a good idea, when you are pregnant, to attend some baby swim classes and see how much fun they are for mother and child. This will help you to overcome any fears which may get in the way later. Your partner can join you in the exercise programme and continue to participate in the birth, bathtime and swimming sessions afterwards. This is a good way to get to know some water babies' and their parents and see the obvious benefits they enjoy.

Physical and psychological preparations in the use of water can begin as soon as you know you are pregnant (or before) and can continue up until the day your labour starts.

Does Water Exercise Combine well with other Land Exercises?

The answer is yes! In fact it is still necessary to practise some basic yoga in addition to your water exercises. Some specific exercises to open the pelvis and relax other parts of the body must be done with the help of gravity on land to be truly effective. This subject has been thoroughly covered in other books by the authors (see page 184). You will find that many of the basic exercises can be done on land and in water and it is ideal to do both. Similarly, walking in the open air is excellent exercise and combines very well with swimming.

Benefits of Water Exercise

Cardio-Respiratory
Your heart is the most important muscle in your body. Swimming and water exercise are ideal for the heart and lungs or cardio-respiratory system during pregnancy. The buoyancy of the water reduces your weight to just a few pounds so that movements that many otherwise be strenuous are easy to do. This gently improves your fitness and aerobic capacity, i.e. the ability of your heart and lungs to transport oxygen and nutrients to your body tissues and also to your baby, and to remove waste products via your bloodstream. The water pressure against your skin also stimulates your circulation and improves your breathing.

Flexibility
The warmth of the water generally increases the elastic quality of your muscles and enhances flexibility of the joints. Some of the water exercises involve stretching which will improve movement at the joints and reduce muscular stiffness. These should be practised on land as well as in water for best effect (see *New Active Birth* by Janet Balaskas for land exercises). In pregnancy, the extra weight you carry may increase stress on your body – particularly the spine, pelvis, sacro-iliac and pubic joints and the knees. Water exercises help to strengthen these areas and reduce the effects of stress. The increase in flexibility improves mobility and ease of movement which helps to prepare you to use comfortable upright positions in labour and for birth – whether on land or in water.

Strength and Endurance
In water your body moves against constant resistance to the water in all directions. Due to the feeling of weightlessness it is much easier to build up your strength without stress and increase your physical endurance and fitness level. Water exercise has a gentle, but powerful, toning effect on your muscles. The 'water resistance effect' massages your whole body as you move, improving circulation and making you feel more vigorous, energetic and alive. This kind of exercise is completely painless and easy to do but, nevertheless, highly effective. In pregnancy, slow movements are most suitable and will prepare you for the physical demands of giving birth and for mothering.

Body Composition
Water exercise helps your body to maintain the right balance between fat and muscle. You should not diet during pregnancy or while you are breastfeeding, and this kind of exercise will help you to burn off calories you don't need and avoid them being stored as excess fat which may be hard to lose after the birth. You can enjoy eating a healthy diet and not gain weight excessively. This is the way to have a shapely pregnant figure and return to your pre-pregnant shape soon after the birth. For women who are very unfit and overweight or uncomfortable during pregnancy, water exercise is the best way to feel light and graceful and improve your health and fitness level without stress. Start very gradually with the programme, pacing yourself slowly according to your ability and you will soon improve.

Posture
Your body undergoes considerable change in pregnancy. The exercises will help your spine to accommodate the extra weight and are designed to reduce stress on the lower back and strengthen the abdominal muscles to improve your posture. Whether in water or on land, always avoid extreme arching positions of the back. Keep your lower back long and your pelvis tucked under in every position. Take care to keep your feet parallel, as turning them out when you stand, exercise or walk will weaken your lower back.

Sleep, Relaxation and Energy
Swimming regularly is an effective way to improve sleep and enhance relaxation when you are pregnant. After babies swim they usually sleep soundly, too, waking less often in the night. If you suffer from fatigue, exhaustion or depression, the energising effects of water exercise can be dramatic. Water can help you to cope with stress or anxiety and give you a greater sense of equilibrium.

Discomforts of Pregnancy
Common symptoms such as backache, swelling, heaviness or nausea can be helped by water exercise. Women with high blood pressure often find that both gentle yoga on land and water exercise can help to keep blood pressure down. Water therapy has been used for healing from the Graeco-Roman era to the baths and spas that are so popular today. Many of the ailments that occur in pregnancy may be helped by hydrotherapy. However, it is essential to discuss the exercise programme with your doctor first, especially if you have a medical problem.

Breathing
A good rhythmic breathing pattern is important for good health. Most of us breath too shallowly and too fast. This programme will help you to breathe deeply and fully. Holding your breath for a short time while swimming underwater helps to improve your aerobic capacity. Your oxygen requirements in water are far less than on land since you do not need to support your body's weight. Use slow, rhythmic breathing, focusing on the exhalation when swimming or exercising unless specific instructions are given.

Physical Appearance and Sexuality
The physical benefits of water exercise encourage a feeling of well-being and a positive attitude and self-image. The sensual and erotic qualities of water put us in touch with our feelings and the sexual instincts which arise during birth and breastfeeding. Water helps to make pregnancy enjoyable – both for you and your baby.

SAFETY Always have someone with you when you swim or exercise in water during pregnancy. Practising with your partner or with a group of pregnant women is very pleasurable. When in a group, a trained lifeguard should always be present.

Useful tips

Water Temperatures
This should be between 78° and 84° F (25° – 28° C). Hot tubs, saunas or hot Jacuzzis are not recommended in pregnancy (although Jacuzzis with warm water are fine).

Depth
Most of the exercises should be done in shoulder-high water. The more your body is submerged the better. If you have a fear of water, then start in waist-high water.

Swimsuits
Wear a well-fitting maternity swimsuit with inner support for your breasts for comfort in the pool. When swimming with a baby, wear a bright, plain colour such as red or blue so that your baby can recognise you easily in the water.

Water Aids
Flotation devices such as polystyrene kick boards or rubber inner tubes can be very useful – especially in late pregnancy when your body is heavy and it's more difficult to float. You can get these from a sports shop or pool distributor. Wax ear plugs can be obtained from a pharmacy if you prefer to use them, but they are not necessary.

Music
Exercising to music is not recommended. It's better to follow your own inner rhythms than to try to keep up with the pace of a piece of music.

Non-Swimmers
The water exercise programme is not done in deep water and many of the movements can be done holding onto a wall. You do not need to know how to swim to do them. Try them in the shallow end of the pool to begin with until you feel more confident and relaxed.

How Often?
Three times a week is ideal if you can find the time. On the days in between, practise some basic yoga postures on land (see recommended reading).

Lap Swimming
This is excellent exercise in pregnancy and can be done as a gentle warm-up before your exercise programme. Choose any stroke you enjoy, sidestroke, crawl or backstroke. Swim slowly, breathing at a comfortable rhythm, and stop before you get tired or rest between laps. The number of laps you do is up to you – so long as you do not get out of breath or tired.

Gentle Jogging
Jogging in water on the spot or across the width of the shallow end is much easier than jogging on land and is energising and great fun when you are pregnant.

Water Walking
Walking in water is relaxing, easy to do and good for you!

Play

It's joyful to simply play in the water so don't be too serious about your water exercise. Remember to be a whale, a mermaid or a dolphin sometimes and to surrender your body to the waves (see page 21). You can do this in your bathtub with a bit of imagination, and if you are lucky enough to be near a clean stretch of sea or a river, make the most of them as often as you can.

WATER EXERCISE PROGRAMME

1   Deep Belly Breathing and Baby Meditation

Position

Stand in the shallow end with your back against the wall. Place your feet about 18 inches apart and make sure that they are parallel. Now bend your knees and lower your body down into an easy squat position with the water at the level of your shoulders.

Touch the wall with your back, lengthening your lower back downwards, by bringing the back of your waist towards the wall. Relax the back of your neck by dropping your chin towards your chest.

Place your hands on your lower belly so that they cradle your baby.

Baby meditation

Deep Breathing

Close your eyes and focus your awareness on the rhythm of your breathing. Observe the natural flow of the breath.

Begin by noticing each exhalation and each inhalation. Breathe out and in slowly through your nose.

Concentrate especially on the out breaths.

Exhale slowly to the very end of the breath, then pause and simply wait for the inhalation to begin. When you feel like breathing in, let the breath come to you of its own accord. Continue like this for three or four breaths and notice how your belly moves when you breathe. When you exhale, your belly moves away from your hands towards your spine. When you inhale your belly moves towards your hands and away from your spine.

Continue a little longer, exaggerating the movements in the belly as described on the following page.

Deep belly breathing

When you exhale, consciously draw in your tummy muscles, away from your hands as if you are bringing your baby closer to your spine. Pause and relax to breathe in. Allow your belly to expand towards your hands as you inhale.

Continue like this until the movement comes naturally. (See meditation on page 42).

Try breathing out through your mouth and making simple vowel sounds such as AAAH or OOOOH when you exhale. This will help you to release sound without inhibition during your labour.

Benefits
When you breathe deeply you are using your diaphragm muscle. Its movements as your lungs fill and empty cause the alternating pressure in the belly. Shallow breathing involves only the intercostal muscles in between your ribs and most of the movement occurs in the chest. The deep breathing exercise improves and deepens your breathing and helps to reverse poor breathing habits (i.e. shallow chest breathing), while preparing you for breathing through contractions in labour.

Underwater Baby Meditation
In the same position, close your eyes, breathe deeply and comfortably and focus your awareness on your baby inside. Imagine what it is like for your baby, floating inside the amniotic fluid within your womb. Imagine the soft, silky feeling of the water on your baby's skin. Imagine the sounds your baby hears inside your body – your heart beating, your voice, the air whooshing through your lungs, the food moving through your digestive system. Imagine how your baby grasps the umbilical cord and is aware of the constant pulse of blood to and from the placenta. Allow yourself to be aware of the strong inner connection you have with your child, now, long before birth.

Visualise your baby's body, limbs, hands and feet, fingers and toes. Imagine the tiny bones of your baby's spine and the rounded shape of the head and the little heart beating strongly. As you breathe deeply, feel your baby moving inside you and know that your child is sensitive to your thoughts and feelings and is already learning from everything you do, receiving your messages and feeling your touch, benefiting from all the nourishment you take in. Surround your baby with radiant white light and loving, welcoming thoughts and feelings before you begin the exercise programme (see also meditation page 42).

Now, take a deep breath, hold it and relax and float freely, or swim, with your head underwater, as if in the womb yourself, for a moment or two before you continue the exercise programme. Try blowing bubbles underwater slowly as you exhale and then come up to inhale.

Partner
Position yourself behind your partner against the wall for deep breathing and baby meditation so that her back is supported against your body. Cradle her in

your arms with both your hands placed gently on her lower belly.

Benefits
This meditation enhances your awareness of your baby and encourages communication and well-being before birth.

2   Circle Breath

Starting Position
Stand in chest-high water away from the edge of the pool.
    Place your feet about two feet apart and parallel.
    Find your balance.
    Tuck your pelvis under your belly to relax your lower back.
    Relax your arms.

Starting position for circle breath

Movement
Warm up by rolling your neck and head around in big, loose circles, keeping your body still. Do three or four complete circles in each direction, releasing any tension in your neck, and come back to the centre ready to begin.

1   Breathe out slowly through your mouth and in through your nose. To start, place your hands together in the prayer position with the palms and fingers touching, an inch or so away from your chest (see photograph).

Exhale, bend knees and lower
arms
Inhale, straighten knees and
raise arms

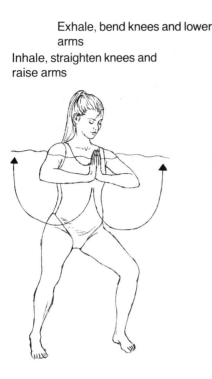

Become aware of the natural flow of your breathing.

2   When you exhale, slowly lower your hands to touch the bottom of an imaginary circle. At the same time, keep your lower back long, bend your knees and lower your body into a wide squat.

3   When you inhale, slowly raise your arms out sideways, describing a wide circle, and straighten your knees into the standing position. Touch your palms together softly at the top of the circle. As you begin to exhale again, lower your arms slowly down the front of your body and bend your knees until you touch the bottom of the circle. Continue the movement very slowly and gracefully, breathing out, lowering your arms and bending on the way down and standing up as you raise your arms and inhale. Complete a few circles in a continuous rhythm and then relax. Release your neck by looking round over your left and right shoulders alternately. As your fitness level improves take this exercise up to ten circles.

Benefits
This exercise increases chest capacity and improves your breathing. It releases and relaxes your neck and shoulders and the muscles that support your breasts. It is calming and centering.

3   Water Wings

Starting Position

Stand or squat away from the edge of the pool with the water up to your shoulders.

Place your feet about two feet apart with feet parallel.

Tuck your pelvis under to lengthen and relax your lower back and make sure you keep it like this throughout the exercise.

Extend your arms out in front of you with elbows straight and place your palms together.

Keep your arms at shoulder height just under the water surface.

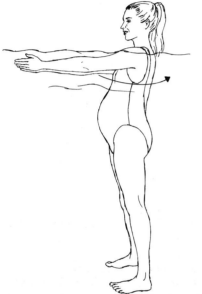

Starting position for water wings

Movement

Breathe in and slowly bring your arms back in a wide circle as far as you can without straining. Stay there and breathe out and in once or twice, feeling your chest expand across the front and your shoulder blades coming together in centre of your back (see next page for back position).

Breathe out and bring your arms forward slowly to the starting position.

Repeat three or four times, building up to ten times. Do this on your own or with a partner.

Partner

Position yourself behind your partner and start by massaging her neck and shoulders in the water. Then move and breathe along with her for the first part of the exercise (see photo). At the end, support her wrists and bring them

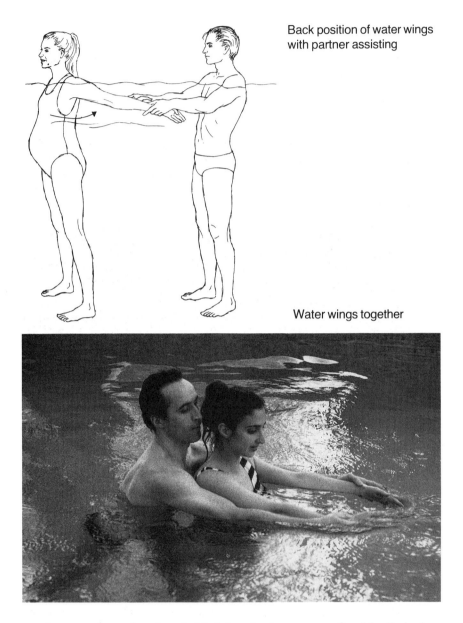

Back position of water wings
with partner assisting

Water wings together

gently towards each other behind her back to a comfortable limit (see drawing), keeping the arms close to the surface of the water. Hold in position while she breathes comfortably for a few moments and then release. Repeat three or four times.

Benefits
This exercise releases tension in the neck, shoulders, arms and upper back. It opens the front of the chest across the breast bone, increases chest capacity, improving breathing and support for the breasts.

4   Side Stretch

Starting Position
Stand in chest-deep water an arms length away from the wall. Place your feet together and keep them parallel with the side of your left foot in line with the wall. Hold onto the side with your left hand, keeping your arm straight. Extend your right arm out sideways with the palm up and let it float softly on the water surface.

Side stretch

Movement
1   Keeping your feet and arms in position, gently dip your hips sideways towards the wall.
2   Now exhale and slowly swing your hips away from the wall and at the same time lean over sideways to the left raising your right arm up gently over your head towards the wall. Avoid straining or leaning forward as you bend (see photograph).
3   Inhale, bringing your right arm down again slowly to the water's surface while swinging your hips in towards the wall. Alternate these movements

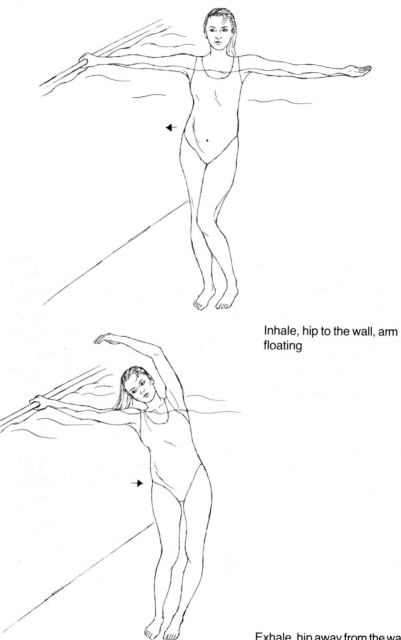

Inhale, hip to the wall, arm floating

Exhale, hip away from the wall, arm up and over

in a continuous rhythmic motion. Continue slowly, repeating the movements gracefully without straining, three or four times, building up to ten times with practice.

Now turn around and repeat on the other side.

Partner
Face your partner and do this exercise together.

Benefits
These movements stretch the side of the body, making more space for your baby. Good for the waistline before and after birth. Increases chest capacity and improves breathing, while strengthening your arm muscles and releasing tension in the neck and shoulders.

5   Leg Exercises

i   *SIDE LIFTS AND SWINGS*

Side lift

Leg to the side

Leg in front

Leg to the side, and back

Starting Position
Stand in waist-high water an arms length away from the wall and hold onto the
edge with your left hand.

Place your feet together making sure they are parallel, with the side of your
left foot in line with the wall.

Movements
a *Side Lifts*
1 Standing on your left (inner) leg, lift your right (outer) leg to the side as
   high as possible.
2 Now lower it downwards in front of the supporting leg, bringing the foot
   towards the wall.
3 Lift it out to the side again and lower it behind the supporting leg.
4 Repeat these movements, alternating front and back three or four times in
   a continuous rhythm, building up to ten times with practice.
   Turn around and repeat with the other leg.
b *Swings* (see drawings overleaf)
In the same starting position as the side lift, stand on your left leg and hold on
to the side with your left hand, with your right hand free or on your right hip.
Swing your right leg from the hip joint and raise it forward and up as high as
possible, keeping your trunk upright. Now, from the hip joint, swing your
right leg backwards and up as high as possible. Alternate these movements
forward and back in a continuous rhythm three or four times, building up to
ten times with practice.
   Change legs and repeat on the other side.

Swing leg forward and up

Swing leg back and up

ii LEG AND ANKLE CIRCLES
Starting Position
This time, stand in waist-high water with your back to the wall and your feet apart. Hold on to the edge with your hands. Make sure that your feet are parallel to each other and making a 90° angle to the pool wall, with your heels facing the wall.

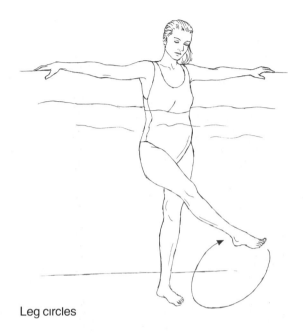

Leg circles

Movements
a   Leg Circles
Stand on your left leg and raise your right. Moving from the hip joint, keep your right leg straight and describe a large circle (at least two feet), in a clockwise direction three or four times. Then repeat in an anti-clockwise direction.

Now change legs and repeat on the other side. Build up to ten circles with practice.

Benefits
These movements exercise the leg muscles and hip joints, improving muscle tone and movement without any strain.

b   Ankle Circles (not illustrated)
In the same position, raise your right leg and rotate your right ankle in a circular motion, first clockwise and then anti-clockwise up to ten times. Now point your toes and then extend your heel and keep alternating up to ten times.

Change legs and repeat on the left.

Benefits
These movements increase flexibility of the ankles and improve circulation and venous return to the upper body. They help to improve posture and make squatting easier.

6   Pelvic Rock'n'Roll

Starting Position
Stand in chest high water, facing the wall. Hold onto the edge of the pool with both hands. Keep your arms straight and place your feet about 18 inches apart and parallel to each other, with the toes pointing towards the wall. Bend your knees slightly, keeping your back straight.

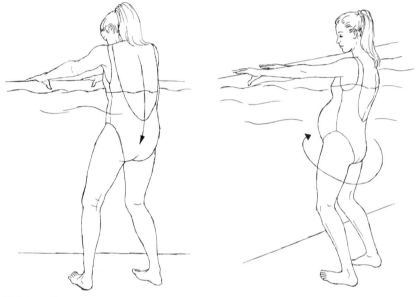

Pelvic rock

Pelvic roll

Movement
a   *Rocking*
Exhale and lengthen your lower back, tucking your pelvis under. At the same time, relax your neck and let your head drop forward towards your chest so that your back is beautifully rounded. Now inhale and release, coming back to the centre, straightening your spine. Alternate these movements in a continuous rhythm and avoid hollowing or arching your lower back when you release. Repeat up to ten times.
b   *Rolling*
In the same position, check that your feet are still parallel and now roll your pelvis round in a circle like a belly dancer. Do up to ten circles and then reverse and roll in the other direction. Try this exercise holding on to the edge in the kneeling position in shallow water as you may want to do it kneeling during your labour.

Benefits
These movements strengthen your lower back and thighs and help to prepare you for moving underwater during contractions in labour. They increase pelvic mobility and the release of tension in the pelvic area. The circular movements are soothing for your baby.

7 Thigh Stretch

Starting Position
Stand in chest-high water facing the pool wall. Hold onto the edge with your left hand.

Keep your arm straight. Place your feet together and parallel to each other with your toes pointing towards the wall.

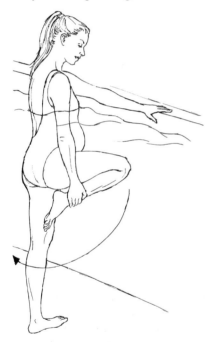

Starting position for thigh stretch

Movement
Stand on your left leg, keeping the foot facing forward towards the wall.
1   Bend your right knee up towards your chest, and hold the ankle with your right hand.
2   Holding your ankle, gently swing your knee down and back, lifting your foot up behind you until you begin to feel an enjoyable stretch in your

Thigh stretch

front thigh muscle. Go as high as you can manage without straining (which may not be as high as in the photograph).

3   Still holding the edge with your left hand, hop backwards on your left foot a little further from the wall, then lean forward to increase the stretch gently. Keep your foot facing the wall all the time.

4   Hold for a few moments, breathing gently, and then return to the starting position and repeat on the other side.

Benefits

This exercise tones and strengthens the thighs.

8 Water Tree

Starting Position

Stand sideways to the edge in chest-high water, an arms length from the wall with your feet together and parallel. The side of your left foot should be in line with the wall. Hold onto the side with your left hand.

Keep your left arm straight. Relax your shoulders and the back of your neck.

Movement

1   Start with your weight even on both legs. Then stand on your left leg, making sure the foot is parallel to the wall and not turning out.

2   Slowly raise your right leg and bend your knees. Place the sole of your right foot against your left thigh, bringing it up as high as possible.

1 Hold your ankle

2 Balance with arm floating

3 Both hands up with palms touching

Hold your right ankle with your right hand. Concentrate on planting your left heel down onto the floor of the pool throughout this exercise. Find your balance and relax.

Focus on your inner centre and concentrate calmly on your breathing for a few moments while holding this position.

3   When, and if, you find it easy to balance, then slowly bring your right arm up to the water surface and let it float freely. Then, if you feel very secure, bring both arms up slowly over your head and place your palms together (see photograph). Breathe and keep the balance for a few moments.

Turn around and repeat on the other side.

Benefits
Calming and centring, this exercise increases mobility of the hip joints and enhances physical and emotional equilibrium.

9   Spinal Twist

Starting Position
Stand away from the edge of the pool with your feet two feet apart and parallel. Tuck your pelvis under, to lengthen your lower back downwards. Bend your knees and drop your pelvis, keeping your back straight so that the water is shoulder high in the bending position.

Link your fingers in front of your chest so that your arms float on the water's surface. Relax your neck and shoulders.

Starting the spinal twist

With feet in position,
turn slowly and look
over your shoulder

Movement
Keeping your feet straight, knees bent and hips facing forward, turn your arms
and upper body slowly to the left. Turn your head gently to look over your left
shoulder without straining. Hold for a second or two and come back slowly to
the centre. Relax and keep lengthening your lower back downwards by
tucking under your pelvis.

With your feet straight, fingers linked, knees bent and hips facing forward,
turn your arms and upper body slowly to the right and look over your right
shoulder. Hold for a second or two, breathing gently, and return slowly to the
centre. Repeat these movements, alternating to the left and right in a
continuous rhythm three to four times, building up to ten times with practice.

Benefits
These movements encourage rotation and flexibility of the spinal column and
stimulate lubrication of the intervertebral joints and movement of the
cerebrospinal fluid.

10   Legs Wide Apart

Starting Position
Stand facing the pool wall. Hold onto the side of the pool with your hands
about 12 inches apart. Keep your arms relaxed and elbows straight. Bring your
legs up onto the wall, opening them as wide apart as possible without straining

Legs wide apart

or bending your knees. (Don't worry if you can't open them as wide as in the photograph).

Extend your heels gently to stretch the back of your legs.

Movement
Hold the position for a minute or two, breathing comfortably. Allow yourself to relax, completely letting go of any tension in your neck so that your body is supported by the buoyancy of the water as you breathe into the stretch.

Benefits
This exercise widens your pelvis and increases flexibility of the pelvic joints and hips while gently stretching the hamstring muscles at the back of your legs and the inner thigh muscles. Improves circulation to and from the legs and venous return to the upper body.

11   Water Tailor

Starting Position
Stand facing the pool wall. Hold onto the side of the pool or the steps with your hands about 12 inches apart and elbows straight. Bend your knees and bring your legs up, placing the soles of your feet together, so that the outside edges are touching the pool wall in between your hands at the surface level of the water. Relax your neck and shoulders.

Water tailor

Movement
Hold the position for a minute or two, breathing comfortably.

Bring your pelvis towards and away from the wall in a gentle rhythmic movement to increase the stretch.

Benefits
This widens the pelvis and increases mobility of the pelvic and hip joints. It improves circulation to the pelvic area and relaxes the lower back and pelvic floor muscles.

12   Water Squats

Starting Position
Stand in shallow water facing the pool wall an arms length from the wall. Place your feet about three feet apart and parallel. Hold onto the edge with your hands 12 inches apart and elbows straight.

Movement
1   Keeping your back straight and pelvis gently tucked under, bend your knees and lower your pelvis into a wide squat so that your body is immersed up to your chest. Hold for a few moments and then return to the standing position. Alternate these movements up and down, up to ten times.

Water squat

2   Still holding the edge with your hands, bring the soles of your feet up onto the wall and place them wide apart and parallel so that your body is in a squatting position on the wall. Keep your arms straight and draw your pelvis closer to the wall to increase the stretch in the hip joints and then release into the original position. Keep your neck and shoulders relaxed and breathe normally. Alternate these movements in a continuous rhythm up to ten times.

Benefits
Squatting widens the pelvic canal, improves circulation, and improves flexibility and mobility of all the pelvic joints. It is ideal preparation for birth and can be used in labour and as a birthing position under water.

13   Partner Squat

Starting Position
This exercise is like a dance. Stand facing each other away from the pool wall. Hold each other by the wrists keeping your arms straight. Open your legs out wide and place your feet about three feet apart so that they are facing forward and are parallel to each other.

Movement
1   Bend your left knee (both of you!) bringing your weight over into your left

Partner squat

foot. At the same time straighten your right leg and extend the heel. You will be moving in the opposite direction to your partner.

2   Now (both of you) glide over to the right, bending your right knee and bringing your weight onto your right foot. At the same time straighten your left leg and extend the heel.

3   Continue gliding slowly and gracefully, shifting your weight from left to right, bending and stretching your legs alternately, moving in the opposite direction to your partner. Repeat up to ten times like a dance and place your feet wider apart with practice.

14   Tummy Toners and Kicks

Starting Position
In the shallow end, stand with your back and heels facing the wall. Extend your arms out to the sides, holding the edge of the pool with your hands. Place your feet close together and parallel to each other at a 90° angle to the wall. Relax the back of your neck and shoulders.

Movements
a   *Knee Bends*
This exercise strengthens the abdominal muscles.

1   Start by holding the edge with your hands. Bend your knees and place the soles of your feet on the wall with your back touching the side.

Bend your knees and place the soles of your feet on the wall

2 Now, with feet apart, draw your knees up towards your chest, leaving plenty of room for your baby. (Postnatally keep your legs together.)

3 Straighten out your legs on the water's surface. Hold for a few seconds, breathing comfortably.

4 Now exhale and bend your knees, drawing them up towards your chest again, and drop slowly into the starting position with your back and soles of the feet touching the wall again.

Repeat these movements slowly three or four times in pregnancy. Build up to ten times after birth.

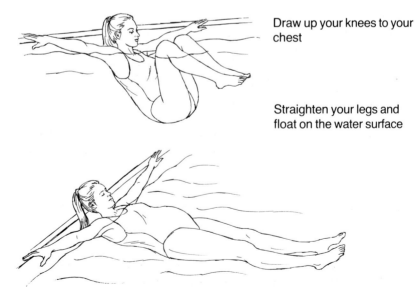

Draw up your knees to your chest

Straighten your legs and float on the water surface

b   *Scissors* (not illustrated)
Still holding onto the edge with your hands, let your body float up towards the water surface. Keep your neck and shoulders relaxed. Open your legs out to the sides as wide as possible and then bring them together and cross them. Continue alternating these 'scissor-like' movements in a continuous rhythm up to ten times.

c   *Water Cycles* (see photograph)
In the following position on your back, hold onto the edge as in (b). Move your legs in a peddling motion as if you are cycling underwater. Continue for a few minutes.

Water cycles

d   *Kicks* (not illustrated)
Roll over onto your tummy. Hold onto the edge with your hands 12 inches apart and arms outstretched. Start this exercise floating in the water on your belly; a polystyrene kickboard placed under the hips may be helpful.

Relax your neck and, if you like, put your face in the water and turn your head sideways when you need to breathe in.

Kick your feet rhythmically for a few moments then relax and turn over onto your back.

Still holding the edge with arms outstretched, relax your neck and allow your head to lie back in the water. Kick your legs rhythmically for a few moments and then relax.

Partner
You can help by supporting her trunk in these exercises – especially in late pregnancy.

Benefits
These movements gently exercise the abdominal muscles without strain and also develop strength in the legs and mobility of the hip joints.

15 Floating Relaxation

This exercise is wonderfully relaxing but can become difficult in late pregnancy. When you feel in need of help, you should take turns with a partner supporting each other, or place a kickboard under your hips to take some of your weight.

Lie on your back on the water, and let go of the side when you are ready. Allow your body to float on the surface of the water. Relax your neck and head so that only your face is above the water.

Find the wave of your breath, noting each exhalation and inhalation. Continue breathing deeply in a comfortable rhythm, focusing on the exhalations. Allow yourself to trust the water to support your body.

Each time you exhale feel your body becoming more relaxed in the water. Relax and release your eyes, jaw, head, neck and shoulders. Let your arms and legs float freely and relax, and release all tensions as you breathe.

Close your eyes and feel how the water supports your body and caresses your skin. Continue like this for a while, becoming very calm and quiet. Focus on the natural rhythm of your breathing. Find the stillness and peace inside and enjoy the sense of connectedness with your inner centre, which will always be found when you really relax.

Allow yourself to be aware of the presence of your baby and enjoy a few minutes of peaceful relaxation together in the water.

When you are ready, open your eyes gradually. Swim to the side and come out very slowly. Wrap yourself in a towel and sit down for a few minutes after leaving the pool, to allow your body time to become used to the effects of gravity again.

Floating relaxation with partner

Partner
Support her trunk in the water lightly to give her a sense of floating. Breathe deeply and relax yourself, tuning in to the mother's energy and the presence of the baby inside her body.

16   Pelvic Floor Exercises
These are done most effectively on land, so you can do them at home or at the poolside.

Easy squatting position for pelvic floor exercises

The muscles which form the floor of your pelvis lie like a hammock across the outlet of your pelvic canal. They are, in fact, three sets of muscles, each of which is arranged in a ring called a sphincter and forms the opening to your bowel, vagina and bladder respectively. They are linked by muscular fibres arranged in a figure eight pattern and together they form the pelvic floor.

This is a vital part of your anatomy as it supports your pelvic organs (uterus, bladder and rectum) and your baby needs to come through these muscles when he or she is being born.

Benefits
If muscle tone in the pelvic floor is weak, the pelvic organs tend to sag and drop down, resulting in problems such as incontinence, prolapse and varicosities and all the discomfort and misery these conditions can cause. On the other hand, if your pelvic floor is too tight or rigid, the birth of your baby may be more difficult and problems such as constipation or recurrent urinary infections are more likely. So, in more ways than one, your happiness depends on a healthy pelvic floor.

Regular exercise will ensure good tone and help to prevent trauma at birth and good recovery postnatally.

During Pregnancy

Starting Position
Squat down outside the pool in an easy squat position, holding onto the ladder, or supporting yourself with your hands on the floor. You need the help of gravity to make this exercise really effective. In this position you are working your pelvic muscles in opposition to gravity to strengthen them.

Movement
a   Contract your pelvic floor muscles, drawing them up tight towards your uterus. Hold for a moment or two and then slowly release your pelvic floor in four small stages, finally releasing completely at the end.
Repeat this twice more.
b   Now try to combine these movements with your breathing. Inhale when you tighten. Hold. Breathe out and in once while holding. Now exhale in four small stages as you release your pelvic floor – finally breathing out completely at the end.
Repeat this twice more.
Now tighten and release quickly ten times.

After the birth
Do this exercise on land for best effect. In the first four to six weeks after the birth do it lying on your tummy on the floor with legs together (put a cushion under your bust for comfort) or on your hands and knees in the 'all fours' position. After that a half-shoulder stand position on the wall is the most gravity-effective position to use for post-natal exercise of the pelvic floor. After birth your pelvic area feels very heavy. Take your time learning to do the shoulder stand gradually in stages. Do only position (a) for seven days then progress to (b). Hold it only for a few seconds and gradually increase the time. Progress to (c) when (b) is easy. Follow the previous instructions for pelvic floor exercises in whichever position is most comfortable to you.

How to get into a Half Shoulder-Stand
a   Start by lying on your back with your knees bent and the soles of your feet parallel against a wall. Tuck your elbows in as close to your body as possible and don't move them or turn your head to the side. Start by breathing and relaxing in this position. Breathe your elbows down onto the floor, lengthen your lower back so your spine relaxes onto the floor.
b   Pressing on the wall with your feet – lift your pelvis up in line with your shoulders, so your weight rests on your elbows, upper arms, neck and shoulders. Breathe and relax and support your upper back with your hands. Do not allow your elbows to splay out to the sides. To come down breathe out and lower your spine gently one vertebra at a time.
c   When (b) is easy you can straighten your legs. To come down lower your spine slowly one vertebra at a time until your whole spine rests on the

floor. Roll over on your side and come up slowly. This exercise also releases tension in the neck and shoulders.

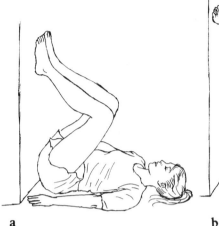

a
Start with feet on the wall and arms in as close to your body as possible

b
Push up and support your back

PELVIC FLOOR EXERCISES
FOR AFTER THE BIRTH

c
Extend and straighten your legs with your feet flat on the wall

5
Labour and Birth

Birth is a transformative experience. While it is the baby who is being born, in these hours a woman becomes a mother, a man becomes a father, a couple become a family, parents become grandparents and perhaps someone is also gaining a new brother or sister.

Many people feel that they can remember experiences that occurred when they were in the womb, during birth and early infancy. These memories are not intellectual or visual, but are deeply embodied states of being, which feel as if they are an intrinsic part of who we have become and how we manifest ourselves throughout our lives.

Adults who undertake a journey of self-awareness through therapy or meditation often get in touch with deep feelings or patterns of behaviour which seem to have originated in their responses to very early experiences including, and sometimes especially, birth. At this time a baby is incredibly sensitive and the first impressions of life are very powerful.

Being born is a momentous experience which involves a dramatic transition from the safety and security of the womb, through the narrow birth canal, into a totally new and different world. For the mother, giving birth is a profound challenge in which she will need to be in touch with her most powerful feminine instincts. Every woman has the resources and knowledge she needs within her to give birth. By making it as easy as possible for her to access her instinctive potential and overcome any inhibitions, we are also creating the best circumstances for the baby's journey to birth, while protecting the spirit of joy and celebration in which the newborn is welcomed into the family. While babies have remarkable powers to cope with and recover from a difficult birth, it is worth making every effort to ensure that your baby's transition is as smooth and welcoming as possible. The relationship between the parents and their attendants and the security and privacy of the environment for birth help the mother to find her strength and surrender to the forces which bring her baby to birth.

The additional option of a pool of water is an invaluable, empowering and harmless resource during labour and birth. However, even if you don't have a pool, water can still help you. The sound of water running from the tap, spending some time in the bath tub, a shower down your back or sponging yourself with a cool wet flannel are amongst the many ways you can connect with the power of water. In this chapter we will explore both the physiological and psychological aspects of labour and birth for mother, father and baby, including the way water, with its special qualities, may be used to enhance the experience.

PLANNING TO USE WATER DURING YOUR BIRTH

Whatever your reasons for wanting to use water for your baby's birth, it is important once you have made the necessary arrangements, that you let go of all your expectations and allow yourself to approach the experience with an open mind. The idea of being in water at this time has a magnetic attraction for many people. Some women feel at their best when they are in water and, understandably, want to share this feeling with their baby in the first few moments after birth. However, while this might turn out to be appropriate, it is impossible to predict how you will feel or what you will need when the time comes. Try not to fall into the trap of setting up a fantasy of the perfect water birth and then feeling obliged to live up to it! Very often, mothers who were determined to give birth in water end up on dry land, while others who had no intention of giving birth in water find themselves unexpectedly in the pool. Be prepared for the possibility that the pool may remain unused on the day even if you have gone to considerable trouble and expense to get one. Your baby's birth should not become an athletic event in which you are under pressure to succeed.

Allow yourself the freedom to choose water as one of the options available to you if it seems appropriate at the time. This attitude may be easiest to achieve in a setting where a pool is always available. If you have spent money on hiring a pool, then try to avoid feeling that you have to use it. Once the pool is in place, it is wise to acknowledge that using water is an option and then let go of any expectations and follow your instinctive feelings when you are in labour.

Sometimes women feel pressured by other people to use water during the birth. Perhaps, for example, in the father's or midwife's fantasy, birth in water represents the ultimate way to be born. If anyone around you has definite needs or wishes concerning the birth, these should be discussed in advance so that you and your baby are not confined by someone else's expectations. For many women, being out of the water and grounded is an absolutely essential prerequisite to giving birth.

If labour is long and difficult there is no doubt that water can sometimes offer a safe alternative to the use of technology. A water pool can be the factor which helps you to overcome your inhibitions and prevents the need for intervention. However, sometimes water is insufficient and other help may be needed.

Water introduces a powerful new dimension and additional medium to help you experience your labour and birth fully. It encourages deep relaxation and the meditative and emotional aspects of giving birth are enhanced. However, it is your desire and ability to accept reality and to flow with whatever happens during your labour that is crucial.

After the birth, as you learn to love and cherish the blessing of your new baby, you will then be able to look back at what happened with feelings of acceptance and gratitude, whatever occurs on the day.

THE BABY AT TERM

The placenta breathes, digests and excretes for your baby. It conveys nutrients from your bloodstream to your baby and excretes waste products.

Inside the uterus your baby floats in the watery environment of the amniotic fluid, free from the effects of gravity.

The strong double membranes of the amniotic sac line the inner wall of the uterine cavity. It lines the inner side of the placenta and the umbilical cord.

The pelvic floor muscles surround the vaginal opening and form the pelvic basin. Your baby comes through them during birth. Muscles of your abdomen, back and thighs attach to your pelvis to provide support and strength.

The umbilical cord is made up of three intertwined blood vessels which link your baby with the placenta.

The uterus extends from your pelvis to your ribs. The wall of the uterus consists of muscle fibres which contract in labour.

The cervix or entrance to the uterus is a sphincter made up of a circle of muscle and fibrous tissue. In pregnancy it is closed and sealed by a plug of jelly-like mucous. It opens during labour.

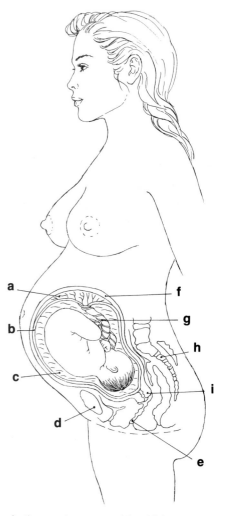

a placenta
b amniotic sac
c amniotic fluid
d pubic bone
e vagina
f uterus
g umbilical cord
h sacrum
i cervix

In the weeks approaching birth your baby lies inside the uterus protected by its muscular walls and the amniotic fluid.

YOU AND YOUR BABY BEFORE LABOUR STARTS

Your baby develops both physically and psychologically throughout the nine months of pregnancy. Hearing, sight, movement, smell, taste, breathing movements, swallowing, sucking, dreaming and waking all begin inside the womb. During this time your baby learns many things. From the start there is no separation between body and mind. As your baby's body functions develop, the psychological experiences your child encounters in the womb begin to influence his or her personality, long before birth. In pregnancy you and your baby are partners both biologically and physically, sharing a mutual togetherness which continues during labour and matures after the birth.

Throughout pregnancy, your baby lies inside the muscular walls of your uterus or womb which is the principle organ involved in pregnancy and birth. At the end of your pregnancy the upper part, or fundus, lies just under your ribs while the cervix or entrance to the uterus is at its base, above the vagina. This is made up of a thick circle of fibrous and muscular tissue forming the sphincter which keeps your uterus closed. In pregnancy the cervix is sealed with a plug of jelly-like mucous. In the last weeks of your pregnancy hormones secreted by your body and by glands within your cervix itself will cause it to soften and 'ripen' in readiness for birth.

Your uterus contracts throughout your life and as you approach birth you will probably be increasingly aware of the practice contractions which prepare your uterus for the birth. In the last weeks of pregnancy these contractions gradually ripen your cervix, so it thins out ready to open or dilate during labour.

Inside the uterus your baby floats in the amniotic fluid, surrounded by the strong double membranes of the amniotic sac. Within this watery environment your baby moves, free from the effects of gravity. The water contains nutrients and maintains your baby's body temperature while providing a sterile fluid full of minerals and proteins for your baby to swallow, inhale and urinate in preparation for feeding, breathing and excreting after birth. It also protects your baby from injury and acts as a shock absorber. During labour, if the membranes remain intact they form a fluid wedge which protects your baby's head as the cervix dilates. The membranes form a sac which lines the inner walls of the uterine cavity including the inner wall of the placenta which is usually attached to the upper part of the uterus. They also form a sheath around the umbilical cord, which is made up of three intertwined blood vessels and links the baby with the placenta. The placenta is a remarkable organ which breathes, digests and excretes for your baby. Its cells are in intimate contact with your blood stream and carry oxygen and vital nutrients and waste products to and from your baby. Soon after birth, when your placenta is no longer needed, it will separate from the wall of the uterus and your body will expel it together with the membranes.

At the end of pregnancy the uterus and all its contents, including your baby, takes up most of the abdominal cavity. From underneath, it is supported by the muscles, ligaments and bony basin of the pelvis. The four bones of the pelvis form a curved funnel shaped canal through which your baby will pass during labour and birth.

The pelvic floor muscles surround the openings to the urethra, vagina and anus at the base of your pelvis. This layer of muscle and fibrous tissue extends across the base of your pelvis from the pubic bone in front to the tailbone (sacrum and coccyx) at the back and also from side to side. The tissues expand and soften in labour to allow your baby to come through them during the final stages of the birth.

Many other muscles attach to the bony pelvic girdle including the strong muscles of the back, the legs and the abdomen and deep muscles of the pelvis. These all help to support your baby when you are pregnant and are used to maintain upright positions in labour and to help you bear down when you give birth.

THE END OF PREGNANCY

In the final weeks of pregnancy you will notice a growing need to focus your attention inwards. The process of opening to the depth and intensity of the birth experience begins with a change of consciousness in which your intellectual rational facilities recede while the release of hormones makes you more dreamy, sensual, instinctive and intuitive.

The length of pregnancy varies from women to women. You may be surprised by the onset of labour before your due date, but the majority of women experience a period of waiting before the baby comes which can seem endless at the time.

The nesting instinct arises strongly in some women and usually manifests as an urgent need to prepare your home. This is the time to dream, rest and sleep, and to spend plenty of time relaxing, exercising and meditating in water, or doing yoga and walking in the open air. Slow swimming is a great relief from the weight you are carrying and will ensure that you approach the birth both fit and rested. It will also help to ensure sounder sleep at night or during the day as your biorhythms change. In the days approaching birth it is wise to surrender to these rhythms and sleep when you feel like it rather than only at night when the increase in uterine activity may keep you awake.

THE STAGES OF LABOUR AND BIRTH

Labour and birth are usually described in three stages. The first stage consists of the dilation and opening of your cervix, the entrance of your womb, wide enough for your baby's head to pass through. In the second stage your baby is actually born and in the third stage, the first contact with your baby takes place and it ends as the placenta and membranes are expelled. In reality you will experience labour and birth as a continuous, finely tuned physiological process which varies from woman to woman rather than in distinct stages.

In the weeks prior to labour, a complex interaction begins between your endocrine and nervous systems and those of your baby to initiate labour. Your

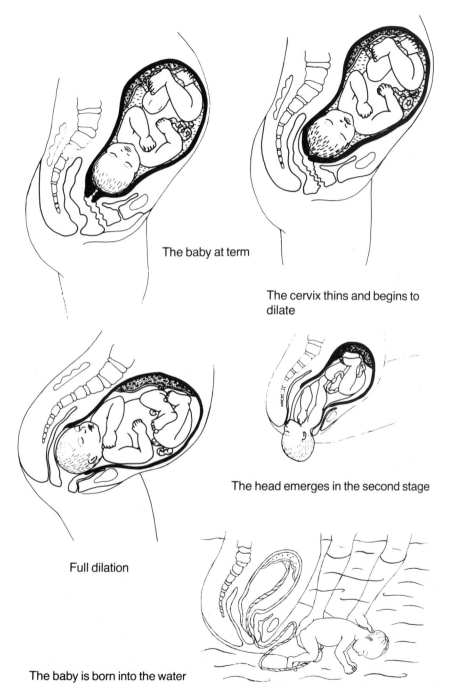

The baby at term

The cervix thins and begins to dilate

The head emerges in the second stage

Full dilation

The baby is born into the water

baby plays an active part in the process. In the weeks before birth your baby's adrenal glands produce a hormone called cortisone which stimulates the release of oestrogen. This is turn stimulates the lining of your uterus to produce prostaglandins, the hormones which soften and ripen your cervix and help your uterus to contract. Cortisone also helps your baby's lungs to mature in readiness for breathing air after birth. During this time as your body and your baby prepare for birth you will be entering 'pre-labour'.

When labour starts, contractions of the uterus are stimulated by the secretion of hormones. The muscular activity of the uterus causes the muscle fibres of the lower segment to gradually stretch so that the cervix thins and then opens. In early labour the contractions are more widely spaced out and gradually build in intensity and length so that they are most frequent and strongest towards the end. While this is happening your baby's head descends deep into the pelvic cavity and you and your baby produce hormones called endorphins which are natural relaxants and painkillers (see page 33). Every labour has its own rhythm and great variety is possible in the overall length of labour. The intervals women experience between contractions varies, too, but they are very intense and close together as the expulsive reflex or urge to push or bear down begins (see page 104). At this time, just before or soon after you reach full dilation, you will probably experience a change as your adrenal glands stimulate the release of adrenalin. This hormone triggers off the 'foetus ejection reflex', as your body prepares to give birth. This time of maximum intensity can be difficult and frightening but it soon leads to the birth of your baby. Your baby's head and body move down through the dilated cervix and pelvic canal to emerge through the vagina. Immediately after birth your baby adapts to the new environment outside the womb and will take the first breath as the first contact takes place between you. In the minutes after birth as you welcome your newborn baby in your arms, the flow of blood from the placenta will cease and it will separate from the inner wall of the uterus. The cord is now cut and further contractions will expel the placenta through your vagina. The important first hours after the birth now unfold. In the sections that follow, labour and birth are described in detail and suggestions are made on the use of water to enhance the experience.

Pre-Labour

When labour is imminent contractions will become more noticeable and more frequent and there is likely to be an increase in the secretion of mucous by your cervix. These contractions are usually painless. They may occur in 'runs' at certain times of day and then stop or there may be mild contractions for several days. The combination of mild contractions and secretion of hormones causes the cervix to 'ripen', ready to open in labour. You could have a 'show'. This consists of a discharge of the jelly-like mucous plug which seals the cervix in pregnancy. It is usually blood-stained and may be red, pink or brownish. A show can happen a few days before labour starts, immediately before or during labour itself.

It is also possible that the membranes of the amniotic sac could rupture so that some of the amniotic fluid or 'waters' are discharged. This, too, may happen several days before or just before labour starts but it usually occurs at the end of labour or during birth. Amniotic fluid is constantly replenished by the placenta and baby even if days elapse before birth. Diarrhoea is common in the last days of pregnancy as your bowel empties in readiness for birth.

Regular contractions will eventually occur and are usually felt in the lower abdomen. They are similar to period pains and when they become strong enough you will know that you are approaching the early stages of your labour.

Alternatively you may feel them in your lower back or inner thighs. This 'pre-labour' may gradually build up for a few days before labour really becomes established. It is as if your uterus is practising and preparing for the birth. However, many women do not experience a pre-labour and go directly into labour once contractions begin.

What to do in Pre-Labour
While ensuring that you conserve your energy, carry on with your life as usual. Exercise, go for a walk, swim, or do some yoga. Eat small, easily-digested meals at frequent intervals and drink plentifully. This is the time to enjoy luxuriating in the bath, followed by a relaxing massage. If contractions occur in bouts then try to rest and sleep between them. You are on the threshold of labour and it's possible that any fears or anxieties you have about labour and birth may surface at this time – for example "Will I be able to cope?" or "Will the baby be alright?" or "Is it normal to feel these unusual sensations in my abdomen or back?" These feelings will pass and may be followed by a new confidence, but it may be helpful to confide in someone you feel close to and make use of the emotional support around you. When pre-labour contractions occur at night, it may be very soothing to enter the water pool for a while, like a kind of rehearsal, or use a big comfortable pile of cushions or a beanbag on your bed and relax, with your body completely supported in a kneeling position so that you can doze between them.

Labour
When labour really begins you will feel your energy centre in your womb and the sensations you experience will become more powerful and demand all of your attention.

Labour is like a sea of contractions which ebb and flow like waves to open your body for your baby to be born. Each contraction begins at the top (fundus) and then spreads down your uterus like a wave towards the cervix. At the peak of the contraction, or crest of the wave, the entire uterine muscle is contracted and then as it ebbs the fibres relax again from the top downwards. There is a break before the next wave begins. Each labour has its own rhythm. In an intense fast labour, the breaks between contractions may be short from the outset and birth often occurs within a few hours. In a long labour, which may last a couple of days, the intervals between contractions may be longer. A first birth usually tends to be longer overall than subsequent labours.

You will feel each contraction begin as a rush of energy which reaches full intensity at its peak and then slowly dissipates. Between contractions there is an 'expansion' or resting period before the next contraction begins. Labour continues in this way, contractions becoming more intense and closer together until your womb is open. Occasionally, full intensity may be reached soon after the onset of contractions.

During the resting phases, the blood flow to the uterus and placenta, which slows down during the contractions, is restored. This ensures that the muscles have energy to work and that the baby is nourished with oxygen. The rhythmic pulsation of the contractions also massage your baby's body, stimulating the nerve endings in the skin which in turn stimulates the baby's internal organs in readiness for birth.

The overall rhythms of labour can be compared to the rhythms of the sea. The water may be still with periods of calm followed by times of intense activity. Sometimes the waves follow after each other relentlessly without a break, like a stormy sea. Towards the end of labour, the power and pain at the peak of the contractions can be almost overwhelming, giving little time to find your centre before the next wave engulfs you.

The way to get through this is to take the contractions one at a time and really let go into your feelings. Allow the contraction to take over, breathe and express yourself freely, using your body without inhibition by making movements and sound as you surrender to the internal opening. The powerful movements of your uterus are completely involuntary. You cannot control them with your mind, so it is best to accept them completely and let them happen without trying to resist or keep control of yourself.

It is helpful to pace yourself like a marathon runner and to rest and replenish your energy between your contractions as deeply as possible, without anticipating what is to come. During intense labour a water pool can be immensely useful in helping you to focus inwards and allow your body's natural rhythms to take over. Water will help you to sink into a state of deep relaxation and surrender. At this time it is preferable to have the minimum of outside stimulation; no disturbing or distracting noises or influences, low lighting and as few people as possible in the room so you do not feel observed and are free to let go (see page 100).

How Does it Feel?
The range of sensations and emotions you may experience in labour is as varied as the moods of a great ocean. There are bound to be blissful times when you feel calm, confident, excited or joyous. At other times fear, anger, irritability or weakness, exhaustion and despair can arise.

Like water, however, feelings flow and it is important to express them freely (and noisily if necessary), during your labour. Allow yourself to cry, to laugh, to curse and complain, moan or sing when you need to.

Physically you will feel the need to empty both bladder and bowel frequently in labour and you may experience some nausea. Retching is common around mid-labour and can be a sign that the labour is speeding up.

One way of looking at labour is as a play between the twin 'goddesses' embodied in every woman. On the one hand there is the calm, loving, compassionate Goddess like Tara, Kuan Yin or the Virgin Mary, who prevails at certain times in labour and during the tender moments you share with your loved ones. On the other hand the powerful demon Goddess, Kali, emerges when you are in your full strength, with her awesome fiery passion to test you and give you the courage and strength to go through the fear, pain and intensity.

Experiencing the Pain
While pain occurs only during contractions, it is usually the predominant sensation women encounter during labour. There are exceptions but for most women the pain experienced at the peak of the contractions in childbirth is profoundly challenging.

Contrary to some women's expectations, a water pool does not guarantee a painless labour. If you are expecting total pain relief then you will be disappointed. When complete relief from pain is needed, other methods such as an epidural are more effective; but many women prefer to avoid pharmacological methods of pain relief (see page 32).

While water won't take all of the pain away, it can help enormously to minimise it, enhance your recovery between contractions and increase your chances of coping without intervention. Nevertheless it is sensible to prepare yourself realistically for the challenge. Try to remain open minded so that you can allow yourself to accept help if you need it, without feeling that you are letting yourself or anyone else down. This freedom is very important. The way women experience pain varies. Some have relatively painless labours, others only feel pain towards the later stages, but for some the pain is a challenge from the outset.

How the pain feels is equally variable. Sometimes it is like a very strong, dull, intense period pain felt in the lower belly and at other times it is sharper, or may be felt in the lower back or thighs (or all three!). Usually the pain is felt only at the peak of the contraction and the subsequent relaxation can be blissful. Occasionally discomfort may persist between contractions. The energy released in your body between contractions can feel wonderful, especially under water, where it is easier for involuntary movements to occur. Many women have reported feelings similar to orgasmic release between the strongest contractions when they are immersed in water. These feelings of release are very special and prepare you for the increase in intensity as labour progresses.

Your body has built-in physiological mechanisms for coping with pain in labour. If the conditions are right your brain will secrete floods of endorphins – hormones which are natural pain killers and relaxants. The level of endorphins will rise as the intensity of labour increases. There are many ways to enhance the secretion of endorphins: breathing, relaxing and sleeping between contractions, moving and making sounds without any control, darkening the room can all be helpful (see page 33).

Immersion in warm water, in the privacy of a calm, intimate atmosphere is a very effective way to enhance endorphin secretion. Sensations of warmth and touch on the skin help to modify the pain by 'gating out' the pain (see page 32). Many women are helped to let go of their rational thinking mind and surrender to the change of consciousness which is natural in labour when they enter the pool. If you don't have a pool, an ordinary bath tub, a shower, a running tap or a sponge bath can also be very helpful and effective.

Endorphins play an important role in all aspects of sexual behaviour, including lovemaking and birth, by stimulating a sense of well-being. In a state of meditation endorphin levels are at their highest. The trance-like relaxation which occurs in labour enables you to sink into the intense sensations and sensuality of your body. When this happens you become one with the pain and it is possible to accept and go through it and to relax completely when it subsides, without anxiety.

Another vitally important factor in relieving pain is having the freedom to move your body instinctively and to make as much noise as you need to release the pain. Making a noise in labour is normal for many women and can be a way of accessing deep reserves of courage and strength.

Energy in Labour
Towards the end of pregnancy your body slows down as if acquiring energy for the birth. The energy demands will depend on the length of your labour and will be affected by your level of fitness. Water can help enormously to conserve energy because it may shorten your labour and also support your weight so that your energy can be optimally used. It is wise to conserve your energy from the start by moving and breathing slowly and resting or sleeping between contractions. Your body will need fluid and glucose to provide nutrition for your muscles during contractions.

If you become short of glucose (sugar) you will feel low and the labour may be prolonged. You do not need a lot of sugar in labour and most women prefer to drink mineral water. To ensure your fluid balance is maintained, drink or sip liquids when you feel like it throughout labour. Water is fine unless your energy is low and you need sugar. Then apple or grape juice, hot water with honey or herbal teas are good. If you feel low, glucose tablets are useful.

Immersion in water will reduce your fluid requirements because it is slowly absorbed through your skin. Maintaining the correct water temperature will prevent overheating, dehydration and loss of energy (see page 164).

Mother and baby soon after a water birth

Floating and resting between contractions

The calm presence and strength of the father help the mother through a strong
contraction at the end of labour

Midwife and mother listen to the baby's heartbeat using a handheld electronic monitor under water

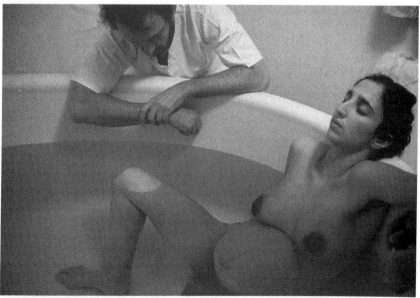

The baby's head crowns

BIRTH UNDER WATER

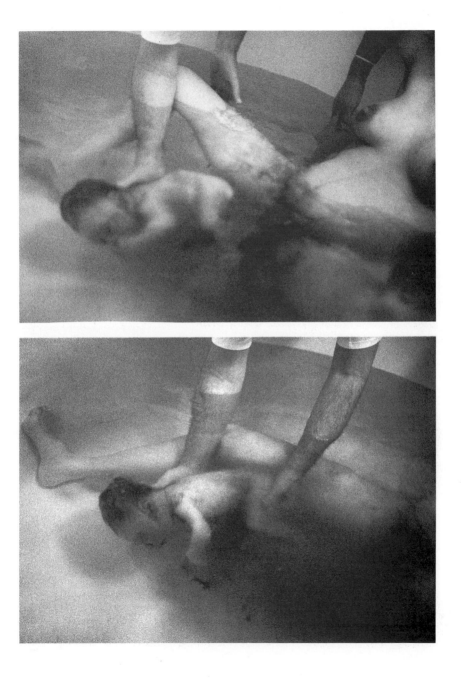

The mother welcomes her baby and the placenta emerges spontaneously into the pool

The day after birth, the new family relax together in the pool

Privacy
Every woman needs privacy to be able to let go to the powerful forces that open her womb and give birth to her baby. To accept the change of consciousness that occurs, which many women describe as 'going off to another planet', it is essential to be totally undisturbed or distracted, secure in the knowledge that help and support is close at hand if you need it. Michel Odent continually stresses the importance of privacy and there is now increasing evidence that birth is easier when this is respected. For some women, a feeling of privacy is possible even when others are present in the room, but many women need to be totally alone. Others feel most secure with a sympathetic partner, midwife or other companion. Inhibition is reduced if people avoid direct eye contact or actually watching the mother. Birth attendants need to be within earshot and, unless the mother needs more intensive support, can remain out of sight or just outside the room (see page 16), bearing in mind that a labouring woman in water should never be left unattended. While some mothers need and welcome them, for others even massage or homeopathic remedies and essential oils are a distraction and should be used sparingly. Instinctively many women keep their heads down, often in a darkened place. At this point, access to water can be miraculous, especially if the room is darkened and the water covers most of the mother's body so she is immersed up to her neck.

Breathing
Being in strong labour is like being in the eye of a hurricane. To cope with the tremendous power of the contractions, you need to reach a state of calm in spite of the power. You will need to be in the midst of the energy as it rises and falls, as each contraction comes and goes, to be able to find the still point between the contractions and to remain centred. While it is a distraction to remember special breathing techniques in labour, the ability to focus on your breathing, particularly the outbreath, will anchor you and help you to find your centre when you need to. In the midst of a tumultuous contraction, focusing on the exhalation as it leaves your body and finding the still point at the bottom of the breath, then relaxing to allow the inhalation to come in slowly, will carry you over the crest of the wave without controlling your breathing. There are several breaths to each contraction. The art of riding the waves is to keep your focus on the exhalations, reach the still point and then let the inhalation come in of its own accord. At all times be in the moment with the breath, and try not to think of what has happened or what is to come. The art of observing your breathing like this will stand you in good stead in labour, after the birth and indeed throughout your life. Regular practise of the deep breathing exercise on page 42 throughout your pregnancy, will ensure that you improve your breathing habits and your ability to breathe deeply.

Focusing on the breath is especially useful if you are tense or anxious. As labour intensifies, the outbreaths are bound to become more noisy.

In very intense labour it usually becomes impossible to focus on the breath. In this case you are already one with the centre and it is best to let go completely

Squatting under water in labour

Kneeling forward onto the rim
of the pool

and express yourself in freedom without trying to focus on anything. Should
you lose your connection with the centre at any time, you have only to focus on
your outbreaths for a while to find it again.

How to use Water during Labour: How long and When to Stay in the Water
The attraction to water and the timing of using the water pool is very individual
and varies from one woman to another and one labour to another. If pre-labour
contractions are intense and there are long runs of contractions prior to the
onset of established labour, water can be extremely soothing. After staying in
water for some time the contractions may diminish, giving you an opportunity
to rest and maybe even fall asleep, thus conserving your energy for the
subsequent labour and birth.

When labour is well established the timing of using the pool once again
shows a wide individual variation. After entering the water dilation is often
rapid during the first hour. It is preferable to keep the pool in reserve for the

Relaxing lying on the side

Floating across the pool

second half of labour when the contractions are intense and the periods of rest shorter. This is when water is most powerful in assisting dilation and shortening labour. However, you might need the comfort of water from quite early on in labour and want to spend hours in the pool prior to the birth itself. In this instance you can go in and out of the pool and alternate between being in water and being on land (see page 103). When the pool is used early, mothers sometimes tire of the water and they may not want to use this valuable resource later on when contractions become more painful and intense. Getting in too early may slow down contractions and prolong labour.

Provided the correct water temperature is maintained and your temperature

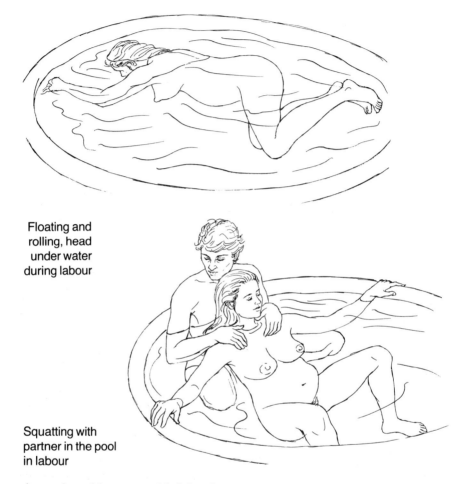

Floating and
rolling, head
under water
during labour

Squatting with
partner in the pool
in labour

is monitored (see page 164), it is safe to stay in the water as long as you like. The depth of the water is also important. The more your body is submerged the more help you will get from buoyancy. However, women's preferences vary. While some like the water to be as deep as possible, others are more comfortable in less water.

When you leave the pool it is advisable to have plenty of large towels available so that you can dry yourself completely. There should also be a heater in the room so that if you feel cold the temperature can be raised quickly (see page 164).

Squatting, lying
back against the
rim

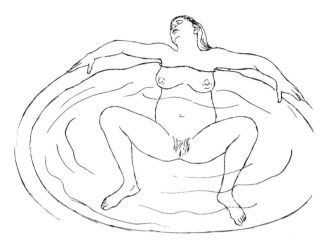

Movements and Positions

There are bound to be times when you prefer or need to be outside the pool on
dry land during your labour, for example, if labour is not progressing well in
water or if you do not feel like being in water. In early labour as your
contractions are beginning to intensify it is essential to make the most of the
help of gravity. You can do this by using positions such as standing, sitting or
squatting during your contractions and resting between them. Follow your
instincts when moving during labour and you will find that these positions
occur spontaneously. Most women use a variety of positions. Some prefer one
or two while other women are more restless and change position frequently.
During contractions movements such as circling your hips or rocking your
pelvis can help to dissipate the pain.

There are many ways to make yourself comfortable in upright positions so
that you do not tire yourself out. It is useful to bear in mind that the more
vertical or upright your body is the more help you will get from gravity. When
standing or walking you may find it helpful to lean forward onto a wall or to be
held by your midwife or partner during the contractions. When kneeling make
sure your knees are resting on a soft surface and use a firm beanbag or pile of
cushions to make yourself comfortable for relaxing between the contractions
and to make sure that your trunk stays fairly vertical. You may want to rest
lying on your side, well propped up by cushions between the contractions. For
squatting, a low stool is very helpful and makes squatting less tiring. You can
also hold onto a firm support or squat between your partner's knees while he
sits on a chair. Sitting on the toilet with your knees spread apart is very
comfortable in labour and for many women the privacy of the bathroom is
appealing. Here you can fill the basin and splash yourself with water if you
want to and enjoy the sound of running water from the tap. For further
guidance on Active Birth see recommended reading on page 184.

Entering the Pool
Once you enter the pool, water powerfully increases your sense of privacy and adds a new dimension to the range of positions and movements you can use. The buoyancy of the water makes it much easier to move and change position and you will find that you will change positions instinctively and movement will occur spontaneously. It's helpful to experiment in the pool or in a swimming pool in the days before your labour begins, and to submerge your head under water at times so that you feel completely familiar and at ease in the water (see page 146). This is a way to block out sounds which are distracting.

You will find that most of the movements and positions you can use on land can be used in water during contractions (see below).

Floating between contractions is a wonderful way to relax, and wetting your hair and going under the water at times reduces outside stimulation and sounds and helps you to let go. There is a wonderful sensuous quality to being in water in labour. It is like reconnecting with the original primal feelings you had in the womb. This is a tremendous aid to surrendering to the birth energy and to letting your body's natural rhythms take over. There is no need to do anything. It will help if the room is darkened and you have enough privacy. With the water as deep as possible you can use your ability to relax and quieten your mind (see meditations on page 41) to sink deeply into your labour. Some women remain quite still in the water, changing positions occasionally, whereas others like to move a lot, rolling from front to back like a mermaid, or a dolphin. Movements and position changes will happen without you needing to think about them. Between contractions you can rest and benefit from the restorative and energising properties of the water. You can sink into its nurturing feminine energy and accept its power to relax you. If you can let go completely you will rest, your energy will recharge and you will enter into a kind of timeless ocean of bliss between the contractions.

The End of Labour
As the birth of the baby approaches contractions will be at their most intense. They will be longer (lasting up to sixty seconds) and closer together so that the intervals are very brief.

This is the peak of labour when the ocean waves are high and turbulent, following upon each other with relentless frequency. The end of labour is usually referred to as 'the transition stage'. You are close to full dilation and your baby's head is about to emerge through the dilated cervix into your vagina ready to be born.

It is normal to feel fearful at this stage. This is the time when you are likely to wish you could get away or have an epidural anaesthetic, when your courage and strength may be at a very low ebb. You may feel angry and irritable or despairing, as if you are exhausted and almost close to death. The breaks between your contractions may give you little respite before the next contraction looms large, like a tidal wave.

It is very helpful to make the most of the respite between contractions and rest and relax deeply, almost sleeping until the next wave begins. This can restore and replenish your energy surprisingly – even though the gaps are short.

The fear which is common at this stage has an important role to play. It triggers off a surge of adrenalin secretion, the 'fight or flight' hormone which stimulates the reflexive contractions which expel your baby during birth. At this time you are on the threshold of giving birth. This is when the powerful demon goddess takes over as the urge to bear down and give birth arises.

Outside stimulation including sound and light or touch should be minimal, as you go through these last demanding contractions without distraction. You will be in an altered state of consciousness, deep inside your labour. Anyone who is present will need to be very discreet and avoid disturbing you, by watching, talking or by being falsely reassuring or anxious. This time can also be difficult for birth attendants and partners who may feel an intense desire to do something to help. However, their calm silence can be a source of strength, reassurance and encouragement as you go through the intensity of the end of labour.

Some women are deeply afraid of the birth at a subconscious level and may experience difficulty in surrendering to the power of these final contractions. Being in warm water helps to let go. Often this intense phase passes very quickly or has a kind of timeless quality. However, if transition is long, you can keep up your energy by sipping water or dilute fruit juice. Most women feel very thirsty when the adrenalin response begins and need to drink a glass or two of water. The bach flower remedy called 'Rescue Remedy' can be very helpful.

At this time near to the birth, the sounds emerging from the birth room tend to be loudest, so there is no need to try to be quiet. You will be in your full power, so feel free to roar like a lioness if you need to. Noise will help you to find the power to assist your baby to come down as your body opens to give birth. Your bowels empty spontaneously as your baby's head presses down and you may need to retch as the expulsive reflex begins. Some women feel shy or inhibited about letting go to these natural reflexes in the presence of other people. It helps to remember that your midwife is used to this and will welcome these events as a sign that the birth is imminent. Whatever happens your concentration will be focused deeply on the power of your contractions with moments of brief but blissful serenity in between them.

At this stage you may feel that you are almost drowning in a sea of contractions. You may wish to leave the water, or alternatively surrender to the power in the weightlessness which its buoyancy allows you. Whether you are in or out of the pool, it is best to use the positions which feel most comfortable, making sure that you can relax, with your body supported between contractions. The water level in the pool should be as high as possible to offer you maximal support.

As birth approaches, many women prefer kneeling. This position helps to give you a sense of control over the intensity of the contractions and makes it easier to relax or even sleep in the brief intervals between them without moving or changing position. At the very end of labour, contractions often slow down and the resting phases may lengthen. The contractions which expel your baby from the womb usually begin around the time full dilation of the cervix is reached. In some women the urge to push may start before dilation is complete and sometimes, on the other hand, there is a break or resting period before expulsion begins. This will feel like a lull, a period of time where suddenly the waves become still and the sea becomes calm. The lull may continue for quite a while before the pushing urge begins. On the other hand you may begin to feel the urge to bear down much earlier. Whatever happens you can trust in the wisdom of your body and surrender to its urges. Soon your baby will be born!

Birth

When your womb has opened and the expulsive contractions are well established you are in 'the second stage', this is the time during which your baby will be born.

Your uterus will contract down powerfully and, with your help, push your baby through the birth canal and into the outside world. This can happen very quickly in just a few contractions or it may take longer.

When the second stage contractions begin your baby's head descends deep into the vagina creating a sense of pressure on the bowel. Further contractions help the descent by pivoting the baby's head under the bony pubic arch of your pelvis. Then when the rounded shape of the head fills the vagina, the crown becomes visible through the lips of the labia. The tissues of the vagina will be soft and elastic as they expand around the baby's head, aided by the natural lubricants of your body and the water.

The final contractions push the baby through the yielding, stretching lips of the vagina and out of your body. There is sometimes a pause when the baby's head is out and the rest of the body is still inside you. With the next contraction the baby's shoulders will emerge one at a time and then the rest of the baby's body will slip out. The body usually emerges easily since the shoulders are smaller in diameter than the baby's head.

If the baby is born into water then the midwife will slowly and gently bring the baby to the surface and into your arms within the first minute after birth. The baby will not begin to breathe until the cooler temperature of the atmosphere stimulates the skin, so there is no danger of the baby inhaling water in the few moments it is still immersed (see page 167).

Should you leave the pool for the birth, then the baby can be gently placed on its belly on a soft, absorbant towel between your legs. In a few moments you will be ready to lift up and welcome your baby.

How Does it Feel?

The exhaustion, which is so common at the end of labour, is often replaced by a new strength and energy which gives you the power to give birth. Many women call for help or have a need to grab hold of someone for support when

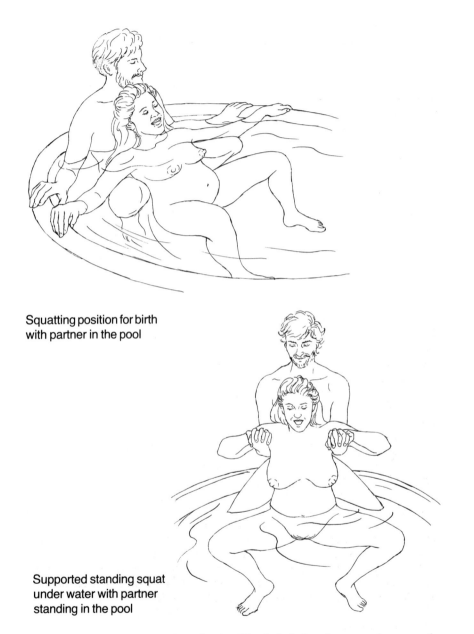

Squatting position for birth
with partner in the pool

Supported standing squat
under water with partner
standing in the pool

the first expulsive contractions begin. The baby's head presses down on the
back wall of the pelvic canal, making you feel as if you need to empty your
bowels. Indeed, a small amount of faecal matter is often pressed out as the baby

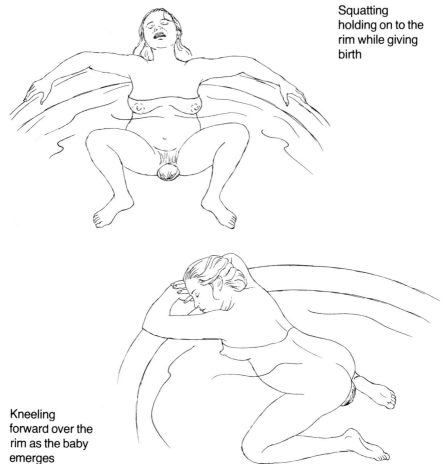

Squatting holding on to the rim while giving birth

Kneeling forward over the rim as the baby emerges

descends and this will not be a problem (see page 168).

The pressure will probably be accompanied by a powerful urge to bear down and push your baby out. The expulsive reflex feels like a huge, irresistable and uncontrollable need to 'PUSH'. These contractions feel very different to the earlier ones in labour. They seem to involve your whole body in a huge and powerful convulsive effort which is involuntary. For many women the pain subsides at the end of labour and these contractions, while very powerful, may be more enjoyable. Some women experience a great exhileration and a feeling that they can work with these contractions.

Other women find the second stage painful and exhausting. This will depend on factors such as the length of labour, size of the baby's head, the fear of stretching or tearing and the ability to surrender to the involuntary power of

Squatting position for birth
under water with partner
outside pool

Squatting standing up with the
baby emerging under the
water surface

the contractions. Fear is the most important factor. The intervals between
contractions will probably be longer than they were during labour so you may
have more time to rest and recover your energy inbetween them.

The expulsive urges are very powerful and many women prefer to give birth
by surrendering completely freely and spontaneously to the rhythm of the

Floating as the baby emerges. The mother's head can be supported from behind

contractions. This is easiest when there has been a conducive atmosphere and sufficient privacy in labour. In this case you would let go totally to your body's urges, without any conscious control, shouting out freely, pushing as and when you feel like it and finally giving birth.

Some women, however, need guidance to help them direct their energy downwards and may need encouragement to make a conscious effort with the contractions, working closely with the midwife. As the baby's head crowns there may be an acute stretching, burning sensation in addition to the expulsive urge as the baby's head presses on the tissues of the vagina and perineum. These moments, as the head emerges, are an exquisite mixture of burning agony and orgasmic pleasure followed by a tremendous sense of relief as the baby's body, wet and silky, slithers out between your legs.

Using Water for the Birth

If you are in the pool at the onset of expulsive contractions there is generally no reason to leave. You can continue to use any position which makes it easiest for you to bear down during contractions and to rest between them. Bearing down is most effective while kneeling or squatting holding onto the edge of the pool. If the birth is easy, sitting or floating on your back may be best. In the rest periods you can float and relax, allowing your body to be supported by the water. You may need someone to hold you, and your partner can do this from inside or outside the pool. Some women feel a need to stand up to bear down. You can stay in the pool as you do so and hold onto the rim or your partner for support or leave the pool if you prefer.

Crowning and Birth under Water
With the last contractions of the second stage the crown of the baby's head begins to emerge from the vagina. The soft tissues of the perineum and vulva stretch and expand around the baby's head as it emerges, aided by the secretion of fluids in the vagina and the softening effect of the warm water. You may want to touch the top of your baby's head when it begins to come through, and some women like to use their hands to assist the birth.

Sometimes, after crowning, the baby is born very quickly in one contraction, but often the head emerges first and is followed by the body with the next contraction. An interval of 2-3 minutes may elapse before the next contractions but the baby is nourished with oxygen by the placenta. First the shoulders are born one at a time and then the chest. Then the rest of the baby's body slips out easily and there is a tremendous sense of orgasmic relief as the baby is born into the water. The head, which is the heaviest part, descends towards the floor of the pool in slow motion. This is quite safe as the baby is supported by the buoyancy of the water.

As soon as the baby is born the midwife will check the pulsation of the cord under water and unravel it if it is around the baby's neck. Within seconds she will slowly and gently bring the baby to the surface, holding it face downwards in the safety position as she passes it to you, to help the amniotic fluid to drain from the lungs.

While under water the baby does not begin to breathe through the lungs, and oxygen continues to reach the baby from the placenta through the umbilical cord. Your baby's heart beating keeps the cord pulsating. Sometimes the mother herself or the father may help to bring the baby to the surface.

Once you are holding your baby in your arms, the face should remain above the water surface so that the baby can breathe. The baby's body may remain immersed until you are ready to leave the pool. The buoyancy of the water can continue to support the baby's body throughout this time, making the entry into gravity more gradual. Your baby's eyes may open under water or within the first moment or two after coming to the surface, as first contact begins.

When to Leave the Pool
Many women want to leave the pool at the end of labour and prefer to give birth on dry land. If this applies to you then follow your instincts and make your way slowly out of the pool between contractions. The temperature of the room should be raised so that you do not feel chilled.

Sometimes the soothing effects and buoyancy of the warm water can reduce the effectiveness of the expulsive reflex and if the second stage is becoming prolonged and exhausting it will be necessary to leave the pool. This is safer for your baby and more practical. If you need maximum effort to bear down and assist with your baby's birth it is best to be in an upright squatting position and grounded on the floor outside the pool. If you have a very large baby or if there is any difficulty in giving birth, gravity effective positions are essential.

GRAVITY EFFECTIVE POSITIONS FOR BIRTH

The supported hanging squat

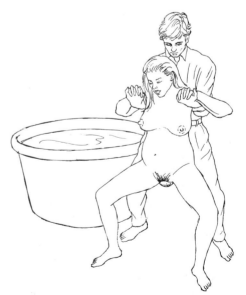

The supported standing squat

The partner squat

Kneeling on all fours is a good position for a very fast birth. This can help to slow things down a little and prevent you feeling overwhelmed. However, if there is any delay in the birth of the head or shoulders, the more upright and grounded you are the better. For women who have difficulty in letting go or opening, it is essential to be grounded on the heels in the supported or partner squat position. When supported like this the pelvic floor muscles are fully relaxed. The baby's head can pass through them easily and tears may be prevented.

A supported standing squat and the partner squat are the most gravity-effective positions and are most suitable when the second stage is prolonged, or if the baby is in the breech position. When the baby is breech it is safer and more practical for the birth to occur on land with the help of gravity (see recommended reading).

Welcoming Your Baby
The first moments after the birth, as you see and hold your baby for the first time, are miraculous. At first you will have a profound sense of relief and then, as your awareness focuses on the baby, a sense of amazement followed by a surge of overwhelming feelings of happiness and joy are common. Often, in the presence of the miracle of birth there is not a dry eye in the room. If the baby's father is present, both parents are united in welcoming their newborn child. However, birth is sometimes so powerful that you may be overwhelmed and it may take time for these feelings to arise, especially if it has been a long, very intense, or exhausting labour. Whether you are in water or on land the umbilical cord may continue to pulsate for up to fifteen minutes while breathing is established. The pulsation which begins in your baby's heart extends to the placenta and is nature's failsafe mechanism which ensures that the baby continues to be nourished by the placenta until independent

breathing in air is secure. It is safest not to cut the cord too soon, to complete the transition to lung breathing before severing the link with the placenta. When breathing is established, the pulsation stops at the placental end of the cord and gradually recedes back to the baby. Waiting until the pulsation in the cord stops is safe and will not predispose your baby to jaundice or anaemia. When the transition is complete, blood will cease to flow through the cord. It will become flaccid and white and no pulse will be felt when you touch it and it can be cut after this. There is no truth to the theory which concerns many paediatricians and midwives that there is a risk of an excess of the baby's blood pooling back in the placenta or flowing into the baby's circulation.

Crying is a powerful way to expand the newborn's lungs. Suction of nose and throat is simple to perform as the baby lies in the mother's chest. Suction is not needed routinely if the baby is held face down in the safety position to allow the amniotic fluid to drain. In the rare instances that the baby requires resuscitation and help with breathing the umbilical cord is clamped and cut and the baby is moved to a resuscitaire.

First Contact

These are the moments you have waited for. Now you can hold your baby in your arms, look into his eyes, gently stroke his body and welcome him into the family, sharing the joy and emotion with those who are present. Your baby will open his eyes and begin to take in the flood of new sensations, secure against the warmth and closeness of your body. You will see how much your baby knows and understands as you gaze into his eyes in the minutes after birth.

First contact takes place on many levels at once, as you touch, smell and see your baby for the first time. The baby's skin may be covered in a creamy substance called vernix which protects the skin from water and from the change in temperature. It will be absorbed soon after the birth. The velvety softness of your baby's skin and the warm sweet smells of the newborn are unique, and will delight your senses.

In the pool, you can relax and welcome your baby remaining in the water. The kneeling position or sitting with your back supported is usually most comfortable for holding your baby in the pool and sitting upright is best on land. In the first ten to fifteen minutes after the birth your baby will be learning to breathe air into the lungs. Once breathing is established contact with the breast begins. The room temperature or, if you have given birth under water, the temperature of the water, should be warm so that the baby doesn't lose heat, and lights should be dim.

First Sucking

The baby is born with a natural reflex to find the breast which is called the 'rooting reflex'. When the nipple touches his cheek or the side of his mouth, he will turn towards it, attracted also by the smell of your body and breasts.

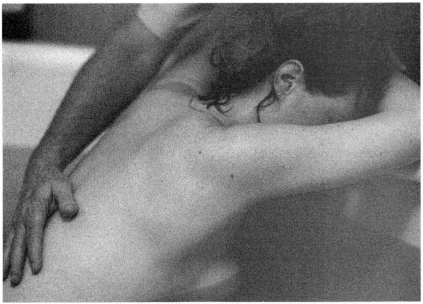

Head down, the mother sinks deep into herself during her first labour

In the calm and darkened birthing room, warm water helps to ease the pain during an intense contraction

The mother has left the water. She cries out freely and in doing so she finds the power to give birth

Some babies will be interested in feeding soon after birth, while others are content to make contact with the breast by licking or smelling and will latch on a little later. It's a good idea to try to latch the baby onto the breast within the first half hour or so, making sure the baby takes both the nipple and part of the surrounding areola into the mouth to prevent nipple soreness.

Hold your baby close to you and turn his body to face yours belly to belly so that the head is facing the nipple and it is easy to open his mouth and latch onto the breast when he is ready. Allow the baby to suck without limitation on the first breast and start on the other side at the next feed. The first feed may take place in water or on land.

Expulsion of the Placenta

First sucking or contact with the breast will stimulate further contractions of the uterus. These contractions or 'after pains' make the placenta separate from the wall of the uterus ready to be expelled with the membranes.

It may be recommended to leave the pool to deliver the placenta, but there are no special risks involved in delivering the placenta under water. In this case the cord can be clamped and cut and you can then leave the pool when you are ready. If you feel faint, if bleeding is excessive or if the baby is unsettled in the water, you will need to leave the pool earlier. It is helpful for you and your partner to know beforehand that the water usually gets quite bloody at this stage. Some blood loss after birth is normal and the blood tends to spread

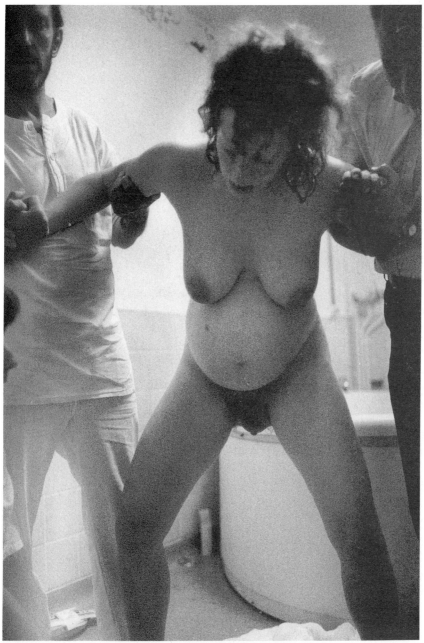

Standing up, supported on either side, the baby's head crowns

The baby is born with the membrane in one contraction

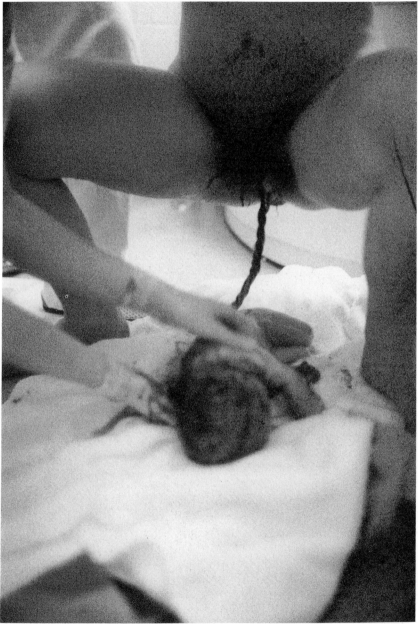

The midwife places the baby down gently onto an absorbent towel in the safety position

Meeting and touching – the moment after birth. Full of emotion the parents see their newborn for the first time

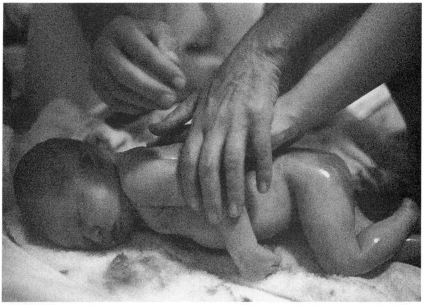

Loving hands of mother and father gently caress her velvet skin

The father cuts the umbilical cord after the placenta has emerged

rapidly throughout the volume of the water.

Squatting, kneeling, or even standing are useful positions to assist the expulsion of the placenta. The cord can be cut after the placenta is delivered. Once the placenta is out you will want to rest and relax with your baby. Your midwife will eventually need to examine your vagina to see if there is a tear or if stitches are necessary. You will need to leave the water to be examined. If this is the case then you may need a local anaesthetic while this is done. Burning, discomfort or pain in the vagina or anus is common in the first hours after the birth, but usually the baby is a wonderful distraction. Sucking will stimulate the uterus to contract and at first the after-pains are intense but lessen over time. They help your uterus to retract and return to its pre-pregnant size. Bathing in warm water will help to soothe discomfort in the vaginal area and sooth after pains.

Recovering and Resting after the Birth
Many mothers enjoy taking a bath with the baby before getting into bed. On the other hand you may want to re-enter the pool if it is easy to change the water. If you gave birth on land this can be a perfect time to use the pool. Sometimes mothers feel faint after the birth and in this case bathing should be delayed (page 171). There is no danger of water entering the uterine cavity through the vagina (page 170). The vaginal walls touch one another and water cannot pass through. If you have had stitches it is recommended to bathe in water. Your birth attendants should escort you in and out of the pool to ensure your safety.

Many parents find these moments spent in warm water with their newborn baby profoundly enjoyable. Fathers often enjoy entering the pool at this time. The baby relaxes, wide-eyed, in the water and it is miraculous to watch the baby's body opening out and extending from the foetal position, caressed and supported by the buoyancy of the water, as he gazes around in wonderment and begins to feel at home in the outside world. Breastfeeding may continue in the water with the baby's body immersed.

These first moments you spend holding, touching and caressing your baby, exploring his face and body, welcoming him, are unforgettable. Like a dance, communication between you takes place on many levels at once. Your baby will go through a characteristic sequence of movements in the first minutes after birth. His eyes usually open first and then the fingers will uncurl until the palms can be seen. His arms and hands search the air, touching the face and begin to explore your body. His head turns towards the sound of your voice and the smells of your body and his eyes follow your movements and gaze searchingly up into your face. In these moments your baby gives out his first signals and receives your responses, and the adventure of learning from your example begins.

In the first hours after the birth your baby is likely to be be very alert, aware and calm. Even though you may be physically tired you will probably have a surge of energy and feeling of excitement. These hours in which you first welcome your newborn baby into the family are very precious and special. You will need to be together in peace and privacy to celebrate the arrival and give the reality of the birth time to sink in. In the days that follow your baby will be sleeping and feeding most of the time so it is important to make the most of the opportunity to be together at this time and to enjoy the radiant and sacred atmosphere that follows the birth.

YOUR BABY DURING LABOUR AND BIRTH
During pregnancy your emotional connection with your child strengthens. Perhaps, towards the end, in preparing yourself to meet the challenge of the birth, you also unconsciously prepare your baby. Your dreams and longing to see your baby after the birth may let him know that you are waiting at the other end to hold him in your arms and welcome him.

Labour and birth is a shared experience between mother and baby. Throughout these long and intense hours there is a mutual interdependence which helps you both to get through the journey. Your baby helps to initiate contractions (see page 86) and also plays an active part by moving during the labour. Your movements in turn encourage the baby's descent into the pelvic canal and may also help to calm and soothe your baby.

In labour there will be times when you are totally absorbed in the intense sensations you are experiencing and other times when you will be aware of your baby's presence. Often the psychic link between mother and baby in labour is so strong, that the mother knows that her baby's heartbeat is just fine, or will be the first to notice if the baby is in trouble. This inner connection is strongest when the atmosphere is very calm, quiet and meditative in labour and can be enhanced by being in water.

Sometimes a mother may change her plans for the birth at the very last moment or in labour. Later, when the birth is over, it becomes obvious that her last minute decision was best for her baby. Practising the meditation on page 42 and the baby awareness exercise on page 52 will help you to develop this intuitive inner connection with your child. While it may sound strange when you just think about it, you can in fact talk to your baby from inside and send him messages, preparing him for what is to come, reassuring him in labour that all is going well or telling him how much you are looking forward to seeing him. When your child grows up the story of his birth will be the one he enjoys most of all. He will remember deeply within him how it felt to be born. Knowing that you are consciously participating in his experience will comfort and reassure him during the birth itself and later throughout life.

It can also work the other way and sometimes the mother is reassured by the baby. In pregnancy and also in labour babies are in tune with their mothers and their psychic abilities may indeed be stronger in the uterus and during birth, infancy and childhood than they are in adult life. A newborn baby's sensitivity to the emotional 'vibrations' around him are obvious soon after the birth and we can assume that this awareness, developed in pregnancy, is also present during the birth.

Throughout pregnancy your baby feels your uterus contract in preparation for birth. In labour, regular contractions massage the head and body as it descends into the pelvic canal. The head descends and turns or rotates within the vaginal walls to accommodate to the widest diameter of the pelvic canal, ready to emerge through your vagina during birth.

Your baby plays an active role in initiating labour itself. The size of your baby's head and body, or the baby's position, can effect the length of labour and the degree of pain you feel. The baby's movements, tucking of the head so that the smallest part presents, wiggling and kicking, all assist his passage through the birth canal. The pulsation of the umbilical cord, generated by your baby's heartbeat, provides oxygen during labour and birth.

When you are in water it will come as no surprise to your baby, who has been an aquatic creature since conception. We can assume that as your body becomes weightless and you relax physically and mentally this will effect your baby too. Less pressure in your abdomen, better oxygenation, and greater ease of movement are beneficial to you both. By the end of labour your baby's head will have descended deep down into the pelvic canal. During this time the cervix draws up around the baby's head. Just before birth the baby's face and head are surrounded by the soft tissues of the vaginal walls within the pelvic bones. The powerful contractions of the uterus in the second stage press down on the baby's body and propel him downwards towards the vaginal opening. For the first time in many months the baby's neck and spine extend as the back of the head comes under the arch of the pelvic bone. We can imagine the intensity of the new sensations the baby experiences during these hours. The powerful contractions, the soft walls of the vagina compressed by the tight, bony passage of the pelvis around the head, the movement of the spine from the familiar flexed position. Perhaps the baby enjoys the massage of the contractions and may also experience some fear, panic or pain coming through the birth canal. Like you, the baby secretes endorphins which help to diminish pain and reduce anxiety and fear.

It helps us to understand the baby's experience when we bear in mind that the intense sensations of being squeezed through the tight walls of the vagina, the compression on the head and spine and the impact of the huge, convulsive contractions of the uterus are entirely new for the baby. For some babies this passage is quick and easy and the baby emerges calm and undisturbed. For others it may be more of a struggle. Babies are especially adapted physiologically to survive the stresses involved in being born. The soft bones of the baby's skull are not yet fused and can overlap or 'mould' to help accommodate to the contours of the birth canal and the baby has a greater capacity to survive with less oxygen than at any other time in life. Sometimes the umbilical cord tightens around the baby's neck. The final stages of the birth may take a long time or the baby may be expelled rapidly. All of this is beyond your conscious control. However, your ability to empathise with what your baby has gone through will assist your communication with your baby and help you to respond to your baby appropriately, as you rest and recover together after the birth.

If your baby is born into water the familiar warm fluid environment may be soothing after birth and ease the adaption to the atmosphere and to gravity. Similarly being born into a loving and sensitive atmosphere on land will help to ensure that the first feelings the baby has as he emerges are of safety and welcome.

During these moments of birth a baby is highly sensitive and impressionable. We know that birth is a momentous occasion in our lives. On a physical and emotional level the effects of the birth experience on the baby and mother are profound.

There is significant evidence, from a wide spectrum of psychotherapies, that our experiences during birth can impress themselves upon us so strongly that emotional patterns originating at this time can persist into adult life. However, the baby is helped after a difficult birth if the parents are able to empathise with the baby's experience and respond lovingly. There are many opportunities for healing in the months after the birth and a mother who is conscious of what her baby went through, and is responsive to his needs, can consequently make the most of his remarkable powers to recover from even the most difficult birth. Your awareness of the awesome power and meaning of the birth experience for your baby will assist his journey through life whatever happens on the day.

Immediately after the birth your baby is fully conscious, exquisitely sensitive, alive and vibrant before your eyes. Within moments his body will begin to move and uncurl from the foetal position, his eyes will open and his hands will begin to explore. Very soon the baby adapts to the impact of gravity, having been used to the buoyancy of the amniotic fluid in the womb. If your baby is born into water the transition is more gradual. The eyes open soon after birth and this can occur under water. Seeing first floods of light and colour as vision begins is an amazing new experience for the baby, who has so far only known the darkness of the womb. When you hold your baby in your arms and greet each other for the first time he can see clearly and focus on your face and features to a distance of about eighteen inches (46 cm). Your baby's gaze will follow your movements and your voice, which he already knows, as he begins to respond to your signals and messages immediately after birth. Looking into your baby's eyes is a wonderful and deeply moving experience. There is a kind of recognition between parents and baby even though you are seeing each other for the first time.

Hearing develops early in the womb and is transmitted to the baby through the amniotic fluid. In the atmosphere the sounds are probably clearer and more direct. The baby's ears are very sensitive and he can hear and recognise your voice and begin to imitate the sounds you make from the start. Your baby's skin is very delicate and responsive to your touch and to the feeling of the cooler atmosphere on its surface. You will notice the creamy white vernix on your baby's body which protects the skin in the womb and helps his body to acclimatise to temperature changes after the birth. The vernix will be absorbed into your baby's body. Your baby's head may be slightly pointed in shape soon after birth. This is caused by the 'moulding' or overlapping of the skull bones which occurs during his passage through the birth canal. The head will soon become rounded again as the bones move back into place. The warmth and smell of your body are vivid for your baby who will turn reflexively towards the breast for comfort and nourishment.

Inside your baby's body dramatic changes occur as the lungs expand and the channels in his heart close to accommodate the change from placenta to lung breathing. The pumping of your baby's heart keeps the cord pulsing with blood from the placenta, so that there is a double source of oxygen until breathing is established. In the meantime the baby begins to make contact with the breast which will take over from the placenta as the source of nourishment and soon the first sucking, which he has practised for months before birth, occurs (see page 46). Your baby is beautifully and naturally adapted to use his inherent reflexes to make this dramatic transition from inside to outside the womb.

Whatever you have dreamed or imagined, nothing can prepare you for the joy of communicating with your baby. From the very beginning your baby is responsive to both mother and father and will express a wide range of feelings. Some babies smile within minutes of birth, obviously pleased to be born and delighting in the new world around them. Relaxing and comforted in your arms, whether in water or not, your baby will soon have a feeling of well-being and contentment. If the birth has been difficult your baby may cry or need to express his feelings, as if to tell you what has happened. Some babies seem disturbed at birth while others are completely calm and tranquil. Sometimes the baby cries to assist the lungs in expanding fully with air. If the baby is fretful and restless, getting into a warm bath or pool will help him to relax and recover.

The baby will remain alert for several hours after the birth, feeding, sensing and exploring your body and the immediate environment. This is the time for mother, father and baby to be together and to include any brothers or sisters in welcoming the new baby. After a while he will fall into a profound sleep and it will be time for everyone to rest. The bonding process continues in these hours after birth as you caress your baby, look at his features, marvel at the softness and smell of his skin, hold his little hands and feet, stroke his body and feel the soft rounded shape of his head. You will need to stay close to each other resting in bed and gradually take in what you have been through in the marvellous afterglow that follows the birth.

THE FATHER'S ROLE DURING THE BIRTH AND AFTER

Becoming a father is a major life change. New responsibilities, experiences and challenges will arise during pregnancy, and intensify after the birth of your baby alongside the pleasure and satisfaction of getting to know your child for the first time. You may have to take sole responsibility for the financial provisions for the family and be cast in the unfamiliar role of organising the household and taking care of the other children. While some men are accustomed to and enjoy these activities, others may find the increased responsibility at home and at work quite stressful.

Men's involvement in labour is a new phenomenon which began in the last twenty-five years. The degree of support your partner will need at the time is difficult to predict and your own desire to participate may be more or less than you expect.

It is best to let go of any preconceived ideas about the birth. While you may have gone to considerable trouble and expense to provide your partner with a water pool, be prepared for the possibility that she may not want to use it on the day!

For some couples the close sharing of these hours is very natural and necessary. Or it may be preferable for you to be nearby while your partner is supported by the close presence of the midwife or other women during labour. It is usually best to follow the mother's inclination in labour. For some men it may not be easy to see their partner in pain, and if this is the case, you should not feel pressured to be present. If you feel anxious, your feelings may be transmitted to your partner in labour. If you had a difficult birth yourself or any previous negative or fearful experiences of birth, it is important to deal with these issues during the pregnancy so that they do not arise during the labour, or perhaps you should even be less directly involved in the labour itself.

On the other hand, you may enjoy sharing in ante-natal preparation and look forward to the birth with confidence and realistic expectations. At the time you may feel very relaxed and calm and be able to make the most of the meditative atmosphere in the labour room. Your close presence may be an emotional necessity for your partner in labour, or she may have a deep need to be alone.

On a practical level, you can take on the important role of protecting the mother's privacy and ensuring that she is not disturbed or distracted. You can also help to communicate her needs and wishes to the hospital staff and be involved in making important choices and decisions.

This will be much easier to do with adequate preparation during pregnancy so fathers are recommended to attend a course of ante-natal couples' classes in order to approach the situation well informed.

The practical organisation involved in setting up the pool and keeping it comfortable in labour is often taken on by the father. In this case, it is wise to be well-rehearsed and to set up the pool at the first sign of labour starting so you can be there for your partner later if she needs you. Some fathers prefer not to look after the pool so they are free to be with the mother. Once the pool is set up, maintaining the water at room temperature is easy to do (see page 180).

Your partner may need you to help her to enter and leave the pool, to physically support her for monitoring the baby's heart or internal examinations, and to hold her in upright positions on land or in the water for the birth. Practising the positions suggested in chapter five prior to the birth will be very useful. Some women invite their partners to enter the pool in labour while others need the pool to themselves. There is no increased risk of infection if the father enters the water since the couple already share the same bacterial environment.

It is normal for amniotic fluid, body excretions and blood to enter the water during labour and especially during the birth (see page 168). The blood entering the water comes from the lining of the uterus which has nourished your baby in pregnancy. When blood enters the volume of water it rapidly disperses throughout the pool, so the water may become quite red at the end. When the time comes and you are in a darkened room, deeply immersed in the labour and excitement of the birth, you are unlikely to notice or care about these details.

Many fathers like to participate and share in the actual birth of their child but some prefer to be at a distance and be called in once the birth is over.

You may choose to enter the bath or pool after the birth and share the intimate experience of greeting your newborn baby for the first time in the water. The direct skin contact in water at this time is wonderful and enhances the experience of welcoming and first getting to know your baby.

You may take great pleasure in cutting the umbilical cord yourself and for some fathers this is an important ritual of separation. The cord will have stopped pulsating and has no nerve supply, so the cutting will not be felt by your baby. You will also be able to hold the baby in your arms. This is perhaps the most wonderful experience for the father. In the moments when your direct relationship with your child begins, as you look into each other's eyes for the first time, you can expect to feel very emotional, and many fathers weep openly with joy.

If this is your second or subsequent baby, you will be concerned about your other children, their care and well-being during the labour and the absence of their mother. Careful arrangements need to be made in advance and you will want to introduce the children to their new baby brother or sister soon after the birth.

Bathing with the mother and baby is a lovely way for the family to spend time together post-natally and often the pool comes into its own in the days following the birth. When other children first enter the room it is a good idea to arrange things so that your partner is not holding the new baby at that moment and can give the older child a welcoming cuddle first and then introduce the baby.

In the weeks after birth, when you are settling back into family life with the new baby, many responsibilities and challenges will accompany the joy of new fatherhood. If at all possible it is advisable to arrange to be at home and enjoy a 'babymoon' in the first week or two after the birth, protecting yourselves against too many visitors. Your partner will be totally absorbed in getting to know the baby and will need your help to take care of shopping, cooking and other household tasks. You will probably need to do far more nurturing than you may be used to, to adjust to broken sleep at night if your baby wakes you and to come to terms with a new set of priorities as your baby's needs take first place for quite some time. Eventually life will settle into a comfortable routine, but in the early weeks you can expect things to be quite different.

While you are bound to be delighted and enraptured by your baby, you may also feel irrational emotions of anger and jealousy at times when the baby demands and uses all of your partner's energy. Fathers are often surprised, or even ashamed, of these feelings, but it is comforting to know that many men feel the same. They will become less intense as your own relationship with your baby matures.

While the baby is intensely involved with feeding and sleeping at first, you will find that your baby recognises and remembers you from the start. If your child has a bout of inconsolable crying you may discover that you have the power to calm and relax, giving your partner a welcome break.

As the weeks go by your relationship with your child will develop, and contact between you will increase as he or she begins to be more alert and interact more with people and the environment. There are many ways you can entertain your baby, and in the beginning fathers often enjoy carrying the baby around the house or out for walks in a baby sling.

Water offers you a very pleasurable way to play with and spend time with your child. From birth onwards you can bath with and massage your baby and later on involve yourself in outings to the swimming pool. Encouraging and helping your partner to go swimming regularly will help her to maintain her health and energy and is also of great benefit to your baby or other children.

The first weeks and months will pass rapidly, although they will seem very intense at the time. It is a great pleasure to observe the development of your baby and to notice the changes from day to day as your baby learns and responds to life. Since these days are so precious and cannot be re-experienced, it is wise to try to enjoy as much time as you can together, sharing the new experience of parenthood with your partner.

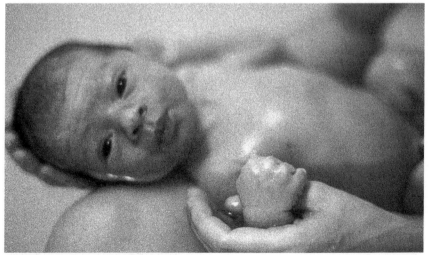

A water baby moments after birth

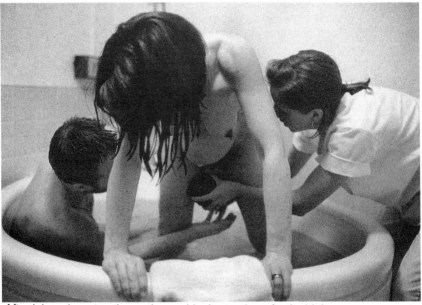

After labour in water, the mother suddenly stands up for the birth

Midwife and father receive the baby together above the water surface

The mother kneels in the water as her baby is passed to her

Skin to skin and eye to eye, the parents share the first contact with their baby

Celebrating the birth in the pool

The first sucking takes place in the water

Resting after the birth

6
After the Birth

In the first few days after birth, your baby will be acclimatising to life outside the womb as you begin to get to know each other. It is best to keep your baby close to the warmth of your body and the familiar sound of your heartbeat most of the time. Being together, both during the day and at night, will help you to learn to respond intuitively to your baby's needs. At first, most of your energy will need to be focused on your relationship with the baby, while feeding is established and you recover from the birth.

Try to ensure, ahead of time, that you have adequate support at home so that you are nourished and taken care of and can devote your full attention to taking care of your baby. Let others attend to the shopping, cooking and housework, and delegate these responsibilities wherever possible.

Your baby will need to be fed at frequent intervals throughout the 24 hours, which means that you will need to rest or sleep when the baby sleeps to conserve and build up your energy.

Adjusting to new parenthood in the early weeks is both challenging and rewarding. You and your partner can expect to experience many intense feelings, highs and lows, at this time. Getting used to interrupted sleep can be difficult and learning to enjoy and respond to your baby should be your priority. Try to surrender to the baby's rhythms. If you settle into a comfortable communication with your baby with minimal conflict, there will be room for everything else in due course.

THE FIRST THREE MONTHS

In the first six weeks the pregnancy hormones diminish and your uterus retracts back into the pelvis, shedding its inner lining as a blood-stained discharge called lochia. The vaginal tissues heal and the muscles and ligaments of your pelvis, abdomen and back return to normal. It may take several months before your body recovers fully. While you are breastfeeding you can expect to retain some extra weight to supply you with strength and energy.

Your pituitary gland produces the hormones prolactin and oxytocin to promote the milk supply and breastfeeding. Ovulation and menstruation are suppressed by prolactin during the breastfeeding period. The more you feed during the 24 hour period, the longer it usually takes before menstruation and fertility return. However, the timing is variable in different women and contraceptive precautions need to be taken if you wish to avoid another pregnancy. While not always the case, many women who are breastfeeding also experience a loss of libido and sexual drive after birth due to the suppression of ovarian estrogen hormones and the intensity of the new relationship with the baby. This can be difficult for the father who is also adjusting to new parenthood.

Getting to know your baby in the early weeks is a great joy. At first, your baby is likely to spend most of the time sleeping between feeds. Sometimes, babies who have had a very gentle and tranquil birth are notably calm and adapt to life after birth with ease so that the transition into parenting flows smoothly. However, this is not always the case and the emotional and physical challenges of these early weeks may be considerable for both parents. There are bound to be times when new parenthood seems easy and others when you will find it quite demanding and exhausting. This depends on a variety of factors. Some babies have little difficulty in getting used to the new activities of digestion and excretion and the stimulation of their new environment and are calm and contented most of the time. However, most babies become more wakeful at around two weeks of age and will cry more as they learn to communicate. In these early weeks there is a kind of 'settling in' period and many babies have a fretful patch in the day when they may cry incessantly. Often, but not always, this occurs in the evening. It is at these times that parents may feel despairing or overwhelmed and most need support and encouragement. However, your baby will gradually settle and the peaceful times will eventually increase and more than compensate for the difficulties. Given time and patience life will settle down and become easier.

Fathers can also expect to have a mixture of intense feelings in the early postnatal period. While the new baby is a source of immense pleasure and pride, there also may be times when fathers may feel irrational feelings of jealousy or anger or a feeling of exclusion from the intense relationship between mother and baby. The father may also have new financial pressures to bear and greater responsibility in the home (see page 126).

Everyone who has a new baby goes through these emotional fluctuations in the early weeks and months and most manage to deal with them. However, if the difficulties are overwhelming, help from family, friends or from a professional may be necessary. Sometimes the challenges of parenting can bring unresolved or suppressed feelings to the surface from your own childhood. If these are understood and dealt with compassionately, then parents may feel doubly rewarded, not only by the joy of having given birth to a child, but also by the satisfaction of the kind of emotional 'rebirth' that follows after resolving these issues.

NOURISHING YOURSELF
- Get plenty of rest. Sleeping in bed with your baby at night is a way to make the night feeds less tiring. Also it is wise to ensure that you rest or nap in the day. It is not necessary to change the baby's nappy at night unless it is soiled or the baby has a rash.
- Eat well – your own nourishment is vital at this time if you are to nourish your baby successfully. Bear in mind that everything you eat goes through to the milk. A good meal and a rest at midday help to boost the milk supply

for the evening feeds. A balanced, wholefood diet with plenty of fresh foods and proteins, spread over three good meals a day, is essential. Some foods you eat may irritate your baby. These include alcohol, highly spiced foods, fruit (especially citrus and plums), dairy products and some vegetables especially in the brassica family. Nicotine from smoking is also an irritant.

- Avoid loneliness. If you are on your own with your baby, seek out the company of other mothers, friends and family when you need to, or join a local postnatal support group.
- Communicate openly with your partner so that you share both the joys and difficulties you encounter and try to understand each other's needs, making time to talk and listen and enjoy each other's company.
- Exercise regularly, taking walks in the fresh air with your baby. At home, practising a few simple yoga exercises, breathing, relaxation and meditation on a daily basis is essential.

As soon as you feel like it, you can return to the water, bathing and doing the exercises in chapter four. Perhaps a friend or your partner can accompany you to hold your baby while you swim. This will help enormously to raise your energy level and enhance relaxation and health. The same water exercise programme can be used after the birth, following the specific instructions for the postnatal period on page 80.

YOUR BABY AFTER BIRTH

In the first hours after birth your baby will be alert and will then fall into a profound sleep and feed intermittently. The new processes of digestion and excretion begin, aided by the colostrum produced by your breasts in the first few days before the milk comes in. This prepares the baby's bowel for digesting milk and has a laxative effect to clear the dark green meconium which is present in the baby's bowels during pregnancy. Colostrum also provides your baby with antibodies needed to cope with the bacteria which are normally present in the environment. Continuous sucking of the highly nutritious colostrum in these first few days in the wakeful periods, both during the day and at night, will help to give your child the best possible start. The baby is undergoing a tremendous adaption, acquiring knowledge and new skills at a rate which would overwhelm most adults. It is not surprising that some babies find it easier than others to get into a harmonious rhythm. Your baby may be restless or cry at times as these new body functions are established. Some babies adapt quickly and others can be quite unsettled for most of the first three months. As the days go by your baby will spend more time awake, increasingly interested in communicating with people and stimulated by the environment.

A baby has a wide variety of states of consciousness which range from deep sleep, rapid eye movement sleep with dreams, light sleep almost awake, awake and calm, awake and restless, awake and crying. The calm, alert state lasts for hours after birth and then occurs for short periods in the next few weeks, gradually becoming longer. You will soon learn to recognise and anticipate the calm times and enjoy them together.

Communicating with your baby is both an intuitive and a learned skill and within a few weeks you will have learnt to interpret her messages and understand her needs.

Feeding your baby
When your baby cries, try feeding first of all. Here are some useful tips to make breastfeeding a pleasure:

● Allow plenty of time – newborn babies feed for hours and very frequently. They need to feed for a long time to get the nutritious 'hind milk' at the end of the feed which is rich in protein and calories. Most babies have a time of day when they have a long sleep and then other times when they feed almost continuously. This normally occurs towards the evenings when you may be feeling tired yourself and the milk supply is lower. If you eat lunch and rest in the afternoon your evening milk will increase. Always remember that continuous feeding is nature's way of stimulating and increasing the milk supply as well as comforting your baby.

● Make sure you are comfortable and relaxed when you breastfeed, using plenty of pillows. Feed your baby in a variety of positions from the start to avoid stress on the nipples. This is the best way to avoid problems.

Breastfeeding Positions

Sitting Upright
a   Place the baby across your lap using a pillow under the baby and good back support for yourself.
b   Place the baby on a cushion beside you, so that her head lies on your lap and body is tucked under your arm. Change sides for the next feed.

a   b

Lying Down

c Lie on your side well propped up by pillows. Tuck your baby in alongside you with her head cradled under your arm and body facing towards yours, head opposite the nearest breast.

d Lie on your side with plenty of pillows under your head and shoulders. Lean gently over your baby and lower your uppermost breast towards her so that the nipple virtually drops into her mouth.

c

d

In Water

e It is possible and very relaxing to feed your baby in water when bathing (see page 145).

When Feeding

● When feeding, turn your baby towards you 'belly to belly' with her body facing the breast. Wait for the baby's mouth to open wide and make sure that she latches on to both the nipple and a good bit of the surrounding areola (Babies feed from the whole breast and not just the nipple).

● Don't time the feeds or restrict the baby's sucking – simply start with a different breast position at each feed. Changing breasts and the baby's position with each feed will prevent soreness by preventing stress on any one area and by draining all areas of the breast evenly.

● Avoid washing your breasts between feeds or using soap.

● Expect some soreness at first. Let your nipples dry in the open air after feeding and then rub in a mild lubricant such as almond oil, a light

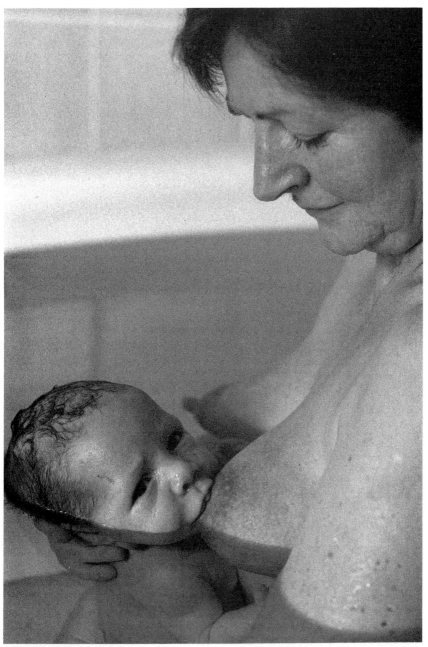

Breastfeeding in water

calendula or camomile cream or lanolin.

- If your breasts are hot and engorged when the milk comes in, try placing some raw cabbage leaves from the fridge inside your bra for an hour or two. This is a wonderful remedy for drawing away the heat and discomfort.

    Engorgement usually passes within 24 hours.

- Wear well-fitted, all-cotton feeding bras.
- Eat well, drink plenty of fluids and get plenty of rest.
- Sort out your priorities and let nourishing your baby and yourself come first.
- Relax when feeding your baby, breathing deeply so that you, too, can be nourished by the feed! Any pain or discomfort will soon ease if you are comfortable and relaxed.

WHAT TO DO WHEN YOUR BABY CRIES

Often, babies do not want to be fed and may need holding, rocking or soothing instead. If your baby does not seem to be hungry then experiment with different ways of calming and entertaining her. Your partner, or other close members of your family, or a friend can help with this and give you a much needed break. Your baby may cry if she is uncomfortable, needs to be changed, is too hot or cold, or is simply overstimulated by all the new sensations she is taking in, in which case going into a quiet, darkened room in the evenings may help. Sometimes we underestimate how exciting being in a normal household environment can be for a tiny baby. Soothing music may help, particularly if your baby has heard the music before birth.

She will cry if she is in pain and sometimes it's impossible for the most experienced mother to know why her baby is crying. Nothing can make the new parent feel more helpless or despairing than these bouts of inconsolable crying (usually called colic) which most babies experience at times in the early weeks. When it happens try to keep calm and centred and comfort your baby as best you can. Focusing on your deep breathing or bathing and massaging your baby may help (see page 142). If you can't cope, hand your baby over to someone else or put her down in a safe place for a few minutes until you regain your composure. If this is a consistent or overwhelming problem, then seek help (see useful addresses). Sometimes the reasons for your baby crying may be emotional and sometimes physical. Occasionally an allergy to something you are eating can be the cause. Watch your diet carefully to observe if anything you are eating could be upsetting your baby through the milk.

Both you and your partner can use a sling to carry your baby from the beginning. Babies tend to feel very secure when held close to your body and may be soothed into restful sleep, both indoors and out in a baby carrier. Hold your baby whenever she cries. Babies benefit from being held and will not become 'spoiled'. They will learn that you are there to support them at times of stress. Observe your baby's rhythms over the day. If there are times when she is usually restless or crying, prepare yourself for this and try to stay calm and centred to be present for your baby without anger or anxiety at this time.

Dress your baby in simple loose comfortable clothes.

A sheepskin for sleeping on can be very comforting for your baby both in the home and when visiting.

Babies love motion, whether being rocked, swung in a hammock or wheeled rythmically.

Spend time each day bathing with your baby. Water offers you a wonderful resource for calming and relaxing your baby and for reducing stress on yourself. Breast feeding in water can help to prevent digestive problems for the baby.

Regular baby massage after bathing can be started soon after birth and helps to relax and soothe your baby (see page 147).

HOW WATER CAN HELP AFTER THE BIRTH

Water can be a great aid in the postnatal months. After all, your baby has spent most of her life in water in the womb and is still perfectly adapted to an aquatic environment. For most babies, being in the familiar medium of warm water is soothing, comforting and relaxing and bathing is a pleasurable addition to your daily activities.

Babies usually enjoy being in water tremendously. It is beneficial to their health and is an enjoyable way for them to exercise in the early months. Some researchers such as Igor Tjarkovsky, go further and claim that time spent in water enhances the baby's development dramatically, since they are better adapted to life in water in the months after birth than on land. Tjarkovsky has observed that the movements babies use in the early months make far more sense in water where they have greater agility. He believes that when babies are taught to retain their aquatic ability from birth they adapt more easily and earlier to life on land and both crawl and walk much sooner.

While Tjarkovsky's ideas fascinate and interest many people, his methods of 'water training' babies are widely criticised because they overide the baby's feelings and are unnecessarily forceful, taking the baby to extremes. There are alternative ways of introducing swimming to babies which involve gentle participation and co-operative play between parent and baby, so that the baby's response and feelings always come first. Learning to swim at an early age is possible but should not be a priority or an inflexible goal. Gentle teaching methods which stimulate the baby's natural joy of learning and need to explore are better than a system of training imposed on the child regardless of his or her willingness to participate. Babies also develop perfectly well without water experience and there is plenty of time to learn water skills. Your baby's happiness and security, trust and enjoyment of being with you in water regularly are far more important than learning to swim in infancy.

However, it is possible for babies to swim before they can crawl or walk. You may enjoy offering your baby this possibility if she enjoys being in water. 'Baby Swim' classes are now a popular option at most swimming pools and there are many specially trained and qualified 'baby swim' instructors. If you want to encourage your baby to swim, it is best to start before six months when babies have an automatic ability to hold their breath under water. This is known as the 'dive reflex' and babies share this capacity with other aquatic and semi-aquatic mammals (see page 152).

For parents who are very confident, secure and at home in water, it is possible to encourage the 'dive reflex' from birth until three months in the bath at home. Others who are less confident, should wait until they have the guidance of an expert at three months. To begin with, there is a great deal to be gained from spending time together, simply bathing in water in the early weeks.

BATHING WITH YOUR BABY

Bathtime with your baby is an activity you can enjoy every day. The main reason for bathing your baby is for pleasure and relaxation rather than for cleaning. If you start off bathing together in the adult bath tub you will find that you do not need a special baby bath. The direct skin contact you share in the bath is part of the benefit and pleasure of bath time. Your baby will also learn to feel safe in a large volume of water from the outset, in preparation for swimming.

You can bath with your baby on your own or, if the bath is large enough, your partner may join in. If there are older children they will take great pleasure in bathing with the baby and this is an excellent way for them to play together.

Preparing for the Bath

If everything you will need is at hand, bathtime will be more relaxed.

First of all, ensure that the bedroom and bathroom are warm enough. Lay out the baby's clothes and prepare a surface to massage and dress your baby after the bath. Next run the bath. You will need a non-slip rubber bathmat in the bath to prevent slipping while holding the baby. When filling the bath with water, or topping it up once you are in, always follow this procedure.

Start with the cold water followed by the hot. When switching off the water start with the hot tap and then switch off the cold. If your baby is touched by cold water it is uncomfortable but not dangerous. However, hot water, even a cup of tea, or contact with the hot tap, can cause severe burns in a baby. Attention to these details from the outset is essential. In the event of an accident, hold the affected part under cold water immediately. Pat dry very very gently and then apply a homeopathic burn ointment immediately (keep some in your home).

Fill the bath as deeply as possible. The water temperature should be warm but not hot. It should feel comfortable for your baby, but not too warm. Probably you will find this a bit cool at first, especially if you are used to hot baths, but warm baths are much healthier for adults and babies alike. Test the water temperature with your elbow (83°F or 28°C is ideal). In the days following the birth, it is safe to add salt to the water, because your baby is used to the salinity of the amniotic fluid.

Babies do not get very dirty and their skins are self-cleansing, so it is unnecessary to use soap or special cleansing agents which dry and crack sensitive skin. Bath oils are not advisable as they make your baby very slippery. Adding two or three drops of pure essential oil is nutritive and relaxing. You can choose from the following oils: rose, geranium, camomile or lavender.

You will need a warm, dry towel for each adult and one for the baby, close to the bath for getting out.

Prepare a soft bath mat beside the bath so you can put the baby down. A large cuddly towelling,bath robe for yourself is very useful.

The bathroom should be warm, quiet and pleasantly lit. Candlelight can be very meditative and relaxing and babies love to look at the flame.

Getting Undressed and Entering the Water

Once everything is ready, undress yourself first, clipping your hair up if you need to. Now undress your baby slowly and give him a cuddle. Holding your baby in your arms against your body, step carefully onto the bathmat in the bath. Lower yourself and baby into a kneeling position in the water and then slowly sit down, lowering your baby into the water gradually, while still in your arms. Very young babies dislike being held at arms length and should always be held against your body when moving. The following are good ways to hold your baby in the water:

a *Water Baby Cuddle*

At first, keep your baby in contact with your body. You can lie him on your chest with his body under the water and head resting on your chest or shoulder. Relax and stroke his body gently, breathing deeply, singing softly or talking to him. Gently caress his head and wet it with a little water using your hand.

Water baby cuddle

b *Baby Swim Position*

After a few days, try holding your baby in the water in the baby swim position. Sit upright at one end of the bath with your legs apart or kneel. With your baby on his tummy, hold him with both hands positioned under his chest lightly with his chin resting on your wrists and head out of the water. Allow him to relax and float in this position. In time, as your confidence grows, begin to play games, drawing your baby towards you in the water, blowing bubbles and making water fountains, dipping your own face in the water.

If your baby accidentally swallows a little water, don't worry, as it won't harm him. React calmly as your anxiety will only convey itself to him. Give him a little cuddle, or breastfeed him, wait for him to recover and then do it again.

Baby swim position

c *Baby Cradle*

Once your baby is used to bathing with you, try lying back and flexing your knees, using your thighs as a cradle for your baby's back. Now it is easy to gently lower your knees so that your baby's body is completely immersed in the water except for his face.

At first just let your baby float comfortably, playing with his hands and feet and caressing his body, and over time as he gets used to the water, gently splash a little water all over his body, including his head and face. This will help him to get used to having his head under water.

Baby cradle

BREASTFEEDING IN WATER

Feeding your baby in the bath is wonderfully relaxing for you both. Make sure the water is as deep as possible and then gently cradle your baby in your arms so that her body is under water. You may enjoy stroking her body or singing to her while she feeds. Take your time. Provided the room is warm and the water temperature is comfortable there is no hurry. Your baby's ears may enter the water and can be dried out after the bath.

HOW LONG TO STAY IN THE BATH

The length of time you spend in the bath is up to you. The baby will not chill if you ensure that the room and water temperatures are maintained. It is safe to stay in for an hour or more. Your instincts will tell you when you need to get out. If your baby is cold he will shiver after he is a few weeks old. Start by staying in for up to half an hour and increase the time gradually.

You will notice that your baby's skin will become progressively resistant to the water and after some weeks you too will be able to remain in water for a longer time without your skin wrinkling.

Most people bath once a day, but it is perfectly safe to bath twice a day if you want to. If your baby is fretful at certain times of the day it is very helpful to time the bath an hour or so before this usually begins and follow the bath with a massage so you are both relaxed ahead of time. Babies usually feed better and sleep very well after a bath and massage.

GETTING OUT OF THE BATH

If two adults are in the bath together, then one of you can leave first, dry yourself and then take the baby. If your partner is around, but not in the bath, he or she can take the baby. If you are alone, then stand up slowly on the non-slip mat, holding the baby. Wrap a warm towel around the baby. Then use one arm to hold the baby and the other to hold onto a firm surface and step slowly and carefully out of the bath.

Dry the baby carefully and place her gently down on the mat you prepared beforehand. Dry yourself and put on a towelling robe. Then pick up the baby and move to a previously warmed room.

Now make sure the creases under the arms, neck and in the elbows and groin are dry. An easy way to do this is to lay the baby on your lap and dust these areas with a light baby powder (calendula or camomile powders are ideal). Dry your baby's outer ears and hair carefully, but do not try to dry the inner ear canal or insert cotton buds. Put your baby's head to each side for a moment or two while drying or feeding. This will allow any water in the ear canal to drain naturally. Make the most of the opportunity to play with your baby as you perform these enjoyable tasks.

BABIES THAT DISLIKE WATER

Most babies have no trouble enjoying water. However, sometimes a baby may actively dislike being undressed and put in water. If this is the case it is not essential for the baby to be bathed. Their skins are self cleaning and you can 'top to tail' them instead for a few weeks and then try again. If your baby has been frightened by sudden exposure or being dipped into water against his will this may be the reason for his fear. You may be able to soothe the baby past this fear in the following way:

1   Wrap your baby in a soft towel and keep it on when entering the bath. Let the towel get wet and gradually remove it in the water.
2   Bath your baby with his vest on for a few weeks.
3   Breastfeed your baby in the bath. The comfort of the breast may help the baby to get used to the feeling of weightlessness in the water.
4   Keep your baby in close contact with your body at all times when bathing.

If your baby continues to dislike water, then don't persist. Trust your baby and respect his individuality. He may not be cut out to be a water baby and will come into his own in other ways.

YOUR OWN FEARS

While some people feel very comforted by water, many men and women have a fear of being in water or of swimming.

Sometimes these fears can be very deep rooted or may go back to a previous traumatic experience in water. Many of us were deprived ourselves of sufficient water experience in childhood. These fears and anxieties may prevent you from benefiting from the healing and meditative effects that water has to offer you and your baby. Some parents are afraid to immerse their baby's head briefly under water, thinking the baby might inhale water or drown. In reality these fears are groundless and will be conveyed to your child. Every baby already knows how to swim. By imposing our fears on them we limit their potential.

If you can try, to examine and come to terms with any feelings of fear so that you can make the most of the soothing and relaxing effects of water. It will help if you use low lighting or candlelight or introduce gentle music into the bathroom. With time and patience you may find that your confidence improves. Spend time alone in water, immersing your head as well as your body until you feel more relaxed. Start very gently taking a breath and putting your head under water for a few seconds and then gradually increase the time. However, it is important to acknowledge your fears and never to try any technique you don't feel entirely confident about with your baby.

MASSAGING YOUR BABY

Touching your baby is instinctive and during the course of a day you massage your baby intuitively without needing to learn any special techniques. However it is possible to increase your natural skills when handling your baby to benefit you both.

Before or after a bath together is a wonderful time for a massage. This pleasurable and relaxing activity is an enjoyable addition to the playful communication you share each day with your child. It can be especially helpful when your baby is fretful or out-of-sorts and will help to release tension as he

Baby massage after the bath

adjusts to life outside the womb.

You can start the day after the birth, or at any time you feel comfortable. Newborns have a very short attention span, so the whole massage should take up to about half an hour. Make sure the room is very warm and free of draughts. Start by sitting comfortably on the floor with your legs outstretched and your back supported if necessary. Put your baby across or on your thighs facing you to begin with, as the feeling of contact with your body is reassuring. When your baby is used to being massaged you can spread a sheepskin or comfortable duvet on the floor and cover it with a soft towel to lay him on as an alternative.

Before you begin, relax and breathe deeply, warming your hands before you touch your baby. Use a light vegetable oil such as almond or grapeseed or a special calendula or camomile baby oil (see useful addresses). If your baby seems to dislike being undressed then you can do these movements through clothing at first, without oil. Start with a very light touch and gradually increase the pressure as you become more confident. Always work with your baby, responding to his reactions. If your baby frets a little at first, sometimes persevering gently may take him through the tension and enable him to relax. However, if your baby continues to protest, then stop the massage and try another part of the body or begin again on another occasion. Once your baby gets used to being massaged he will probably love it and show obvious signs of pleasure.

In this book we will focus on massage for the abdomen, chest and back, as these are the common areas in which tension accumulates in a young baby (see page 184. for further reading). Use your intuition to continue with the thighs, calves and feet and the arms, hands and fingers, head and face. Remember to be playful and to sing, talk and amuse your baby as you go along. At all times allow your intuition to be your guide, using the techniques we suggest as a starting point.

Massaging your baby is very easy and is a delightful pastime. There are no complicated techniques to learn and you will become an expert in no time.

Abdomen and Chest Massage
Place your baby on your thighs face up. Start by using plenty of warm oil and spread it evenly over your baby's body. Begin the massage with the chest and abdomen as illustrated below and then in your own way continue with the shoulders, arms and legs, hands and feet.

1   *Chest and Belly Massage*
Use both hands and stroke evenly with your fingers down the midline of the abdomen from the chest to the pubic area. Then, continuing the movement, separate your hands and stroke gently up the side of the torso as far as the armpits. Circle round over the top of the chest and down the midline again. Repeat the cycle in a slow and steady rhythm for up to three minutes.

Chest and belly massage

2   *Diagonal Strokes*

Using a light, even pressure, run the fingers of your right hand diagonally across your baby's body from the left shoulder to the right hip. Then change hands and stroke from the right shoulder to the left hip. Alternate in a continuous rhythm for a minute or so.

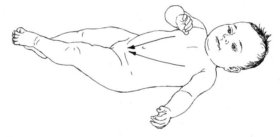

Diagonal strokes

3   *Circling the Navel*

Use your fingertips or your thumb to rub round and round the navel in a clockwise direction. Use a steady, gentle pressure. This abdominal massage stimulates the bowel and releases tension in the belly to relieve colic or wind. Continue for a minute or so. If your baby has diarrhoea then work in the opposite direction.

4   *Percussion*

Keep your wrists very loose and floppy and tap your baby's chest with your fingertips. Start slowly and then let the movements speed up. Babies usually enjoy this and it helps to loosen up any mucous if your baby has a cold.

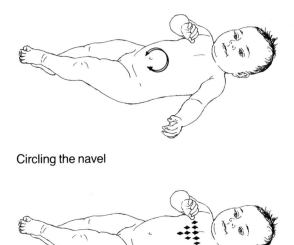

Circling the navel

Chest percussion

Back Massage

1 *Full Back Massage*
Place your baby on your thighs or on a sheepskin face down. Use a gentle pressure and massage down both sides of the spine with your fingers from top to bottom. At the base of the spine separate your hands and stroke around each buttock and then draw them lightly up your baby's sides towards the armpits. Circle over the shoulder blades and down the spine again. Continue in a slow continuous rythym for up to three minutes.

Full back massage

2   *Hip Massage*

Use two fingers and a firm, even pressure to describe a circle. Start below the buttocks and work up around the hip bone and round the top of the thigh to complete the circle. Continue slowly for up to three minutes. You can turn your baby on his side and massage one hip at a time if you prefer.

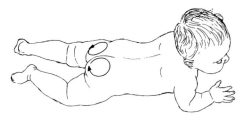

Hip massage

3   *Brushing Down*

Place a hand on each shoulder blade. Stroke lightly down to the lower back and then separate your hands and stroke down over the hips, thighs, calves, off the feet. Make slow, light sweeping movements and repeat for up to two minutes.

Brushing down

4   *Upper Back Percussion*

Make loose fists with your hands. Keeping your wrists floppy, percuss with the little finger side of your fists on the hand between your baby's shoulder blades. Keep the rhythm steady and allow it to speed up. Continue for up to three minutes. This will also help to loosen mucous congestion.

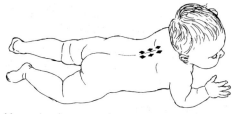

Upper back percussion

INTRODUCING YOUR BABY TO SWIMMING

When you bath with your baby there will be times when you lie together in the water quietly, times when your baby feeds, as well as more playful moments when your baby will want to play, swim, try different positions and explore. You may be quite content to continue with the suggestions we have made so far until your baby is three months old and ready to join a baby swim class. On the other hand you may begin to feel that you would like to start to introduce your baby to swimming. By now your baby should be very relaxed in water and accustomed to the daily bath routine and you yourself should be feeling confident and at ease with your child in the water.

Unless there is this feeling of mutual trust and relaxation in water it is essential to wait until you have the guidance of a teacher before you begin this exercise. However you may begin soon after birth if you like.

Your first swimming lesson with your baby in the bath
Babies already know how to swim. They are born with a swimming and diving reflex which they develop in the aquatic environment of the womb. When a young baby's head is immersed in water the air passages automatically close to prevent inhalation of water. Teaching your baby to swim in water is really a matter of keeping these reflexes active so that your baby, in fact, does not *forget* how to swim. This is easiest if you start when your baby is very young – even within days of the birth. However, the diving reflex is active until around six months of age, so start whenever you feel the time is right. After six months it becomes more difficult to teach your child to hold his breath under water and you may need to wait until she is old enough to play games that get her used to putting her head under water (at around eighteen months). Children who learn to swim at a later stage will soon feel completely confident at home in and under the water.

Once you are familiar with bathing with your baby you may begin swimming with her in the bath at home. If you feel unsure about doing so then it is best to wait for the guidance of a teacher when your child is three months old. However, if you feel confident and relaxed, this exercise will help to encourage your child's natural dive reflex.

It is important to have a calm and quiet atmosphere. Some quiet music in another room or the presence of your partner may help to relax you.

Relax together in the bath in the usual way before you start. Sit or kneel in the water and hold your baby at arm's length with your hands around either side of her rib cage. Look into your baby's eyes, smile at her and then take a deep breath in yourself. Now blow directly in your baby's face, making the sound 'Phewwwww' and she will automatically take in a breath of air and close her throat. Without hesitating, gently lower her, head and all, under the surface of the water. Keep her under for only a second. Keep watching her very carefully and draw her gently towards you and then slowly bring her out of the water. Give her a calm cuddle and a kiss. Repeat this once more and build up to doing it three or four times during each bath session.

Blowing in your baby's face makes her take a breath and becomes a signal between you that you are going under the water. If your baby accidentally swallows some water she will cough and splutter a bit. Comfort her calmly and don't worry as it won't harm her and she will soon get used to it. This is equivalent to the odd bump and fall when learning to walk!

Keeping calm yourself throughout is very important, as any tension or anxiety will be conveyed to your baby. Remember that under water without gravity, your baby's oxygen requirements are much less and she is in fact capable of staying under the surface for over a minute without any problem. However, for safety's sake, always bring her to the surface after a few seconds.

Until your baby can swim she will need your help to come to the surface. When you are familiar with this exercise you will understand your baby's signals that it is time to come up. Some babies take to swimming like a duck to water, while others may cry a little at first until they get used to it. If you or your baby do not enjoy it then don't persist and wait until she is a little older to try again with a teacher.

When you leave the water, place your baby on your lap or on a soft surface in the safety position – that is on her stomach like a frog – to encourage any water to drain from her nose and mouth and cover her warmly.

Cautions
- Some babies dislike putting their heads under water and this should only be done with the baby's full and total co-operation. If your baby doesn't want to do this for months or even years, then her needs should be respected.
- Build up your own confidence in water before swimming with your baby. You can begin by putting your head under water for a few seconds in the safety of your own bath tub and gradually learn to open your eyes and stay under for longer (see page 146).
- **Safety precaution – You need your complete undivided attention focused on your baby when she is in or under water. Even a moment's lapse may result in your baby inhaling water.**

  If she *does*, react calmly. Don't panic and bring her gently to the surface. Hold her in your arms against your body, face down, and gently rub her back until she recovers. Never allow yourself to be distracted when your child is in water.
- Never leave your baby unattended in the bath, even with another child, while you step out of the bathroom.
- After your baby has had her head under water, whether in the bath or pool, dry her ears really carefully. Dry the outside with a towel and then turn her head to the side to allow any water in the auditory canal to drain away, and repeat on the other side. If you are going outside into the cold to go home then put a warm hat on her after swimming.
- Never swim with a baby that has any kind of ear infection or is unwell.

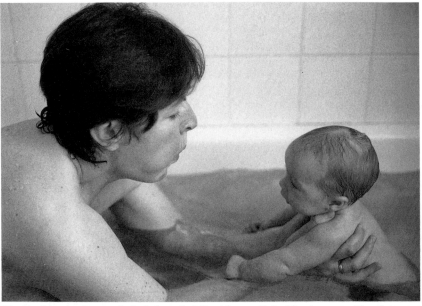

Start by blowing in your baby's face, holding him gently but firmly around the ribcage

Lower him under the water, head and all, for a few seconds

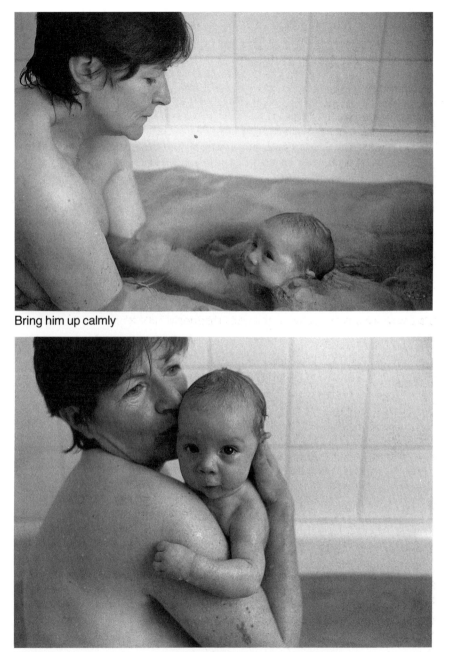

Bring him up calmly

Give him a gentle cuddle and then repeat up to three or four times

Introducing your child to a swimming pool

It is generally advised that babies should be innoculated once before going into a public swimming pool, so around the age of three months is the best time to start. Visit first before introducing your baby to the pool, so both you and she can get used to the new environment and explore the facilities. Make sure that the swimming instructor has been especially trained to work with babies. The photographs below show a typical mother and baby swimming class in the pool.

If you wish to attend a class, you will need to explore the facilities for baby swimming lessons in your area. Some parents are concerned about the effect on the baby of chlorine in public pools. While water without chlorine is certainly preferable, the benefits of the exercise outweigh the effect of the chlorine. Unless your baby has severe eczema or is allergic to chlorine, it is not likely to cause any problems. It is advisable to wash your baby with a mild soap and to shampoo his or her hair after swimming in a public pool to remove the chlorine. Follow this with a massage with baby oil or a mild moisturising lotion.

There are several approaches to babyswim teaching methods and it is wise to observe a few different classes before choosing the one you like the most. If you prefer not to go to a formal class, a great deal of pleasure can be gained by going frequently to your local pool on your own with your baby and holding and playing with her in the water. Some parents prefer to teach their child to swim

A baby swim class in a municipal swimming pool

Under water swimming lesson in the pool

Coming up for a cuddle

slowly and intuitively, and it is the positive water experience which is most important.

The main thing is that she should frequently enjoy the experience of being in water with you in an atmosphere of love and trust. Being with your baby in water enhances her development and enjoyment of life. It is a way to help her expend her energy and to sleep well afterwards.

Swimming with your child is a health-giving and invigorating way to exercise and has many physiological and emotional benefits for you both, especially during the first eight months when babies are less agile on land.

Humans have a natural ability to be in water and this is present from before birth. All babies can instinctively control their breathing under water and very young babies have not yet learnt to fear being in water. These natural instincts can be encouraged and developed. Ideally a mother should prepare for this during her own pregnancy, overcoming her fears, regaining her confidence and trust in water so she can continue to pass on this health-giving instinct to her child.

7

Suggestions for Partners, Midwives and Doctors

The advent of water in the birth room raises many new issues for partners and birth attendants to consider. In this chapter we will try to answer some of the questions which commonly arise when the help of water is first introduced.

Many midwives and doctors welcome the possibility of providing a harmless way to make labour and birth easier, to relieve pain and reduce the need for intervention. After gaining some experience with the use of water they soon realise that the risks and problems are minimal.

While acknowledging the potential advantages for mother and baby, providing a pool and attending a mother who is labouring or giving birth in a pool of water is a very recent phenomenon. Understandably, many partners, midwives and obstetricians have fears for the safety of mother and baby in water. Usually these reservations are groundless and it is sometimes the attendant's own personal fear which is at the centre of the problem.

Water provides the midwife with an extra dimension to enhance her skills in addition to the kind, warm, sympathetic and motherly presence which is so essential to the mother in labour. The number of natural active births will rise and there will be far greater job satisfaction for the midwife. What could be more satisfying than assisting a woman to give birth to her baby using the curative and healing power of water to aid the progress of labour and to help the mother to overcome any inhibitions? The presence of a water pool also nourishes the midwife and helps everyone who is present to relax and accept the ebb and flow of the labour. Access to water in labour represents a very real and important step forward to encourage natural physiological childbirth.

INSTALLING A POOL AT HOME

A variety of portable pools for use in the home are now available for purchase or hire (see page 183). It is best to hire a pool for a four week period so that it is available for two weeks before and after your expected due date. Introducing approximately 200 gallons of water into your home should not be taken lightly, so make sure that the house is strong enough and all the necessary equipment is provided in good working order and that you understand how to assemble the

An unexpected water birth in the bath at home. The parents share a moment of ecstasy as the mother takes the baby in her arms for the first time

pool and follow the directions explicitly. The pool hire company should provide a detailed practical demonstration of how to set up and take care of the equipment. Due to the close proximity of water to electricity in the home it is advisable to have an electrician or the electricity board install earth linkage circuit breakers or trip switches for safety. When you first introduce the pool into your home, set it up once as a practise run to ensure that there are no technical hitches on the day. It is good for the mother to spend time relaxing in the pool in the days before labour actually starts. You will need to be well versed in all the details of heating, filling and emptying the pool.

What to look for in a birth pool
The pool should be made from a non-porous material such as fibreglass or hard plastic which can be easily cleaned and will not harbour bacteria. An opaque, rather than transparent, material provides greater privacy for the mother.

Some pools are in one piece while others come in sections. If a one piece pool is used, it is best if it can be drained through a plug hole from the bottom so it is easy to clean and flush out. If the pool comes in sections, ensure that parts are easy to assemble. With this type of pool the frame makes up the side walls of the pool and the water is usually contained by a double liner made of P.V.C. plastic which forms the base of the pool and fits over the frame (see page 180). The plastic liners should be provided – a thick outer one as well as a disposable inner liner to allow for maximum hygiene and ease when cleaning up. A heater may be needed and a pump and separate hoses for filling and emptying the water are essential.

Size and Shape
A circular, oval or eliptical shape provides a comfortable womb-like space for the mother and easy access for the attendant. The pool should be large enough for the mother to move in freedom and for another adult to enter, in case her partner or midwife needs to get into the water. It should not be too large, however, as a smaller space feels more secure during labour.

The height of the water in the pool should be around 24 inches (60 cm), so that the water is deep enough for the whole of the mother's abdomen to be fully immersed in a variety of upright positions. The edges of the pool should be smooth and rounded for comfort, or padding should be provided. If the disposable liner system is used, then foam padding can be inserted between the inner and outer liners to form a comfortable cushion around the rim for leaning on. (See page 163 for more details on pool design.)

Water Heating and Pumping Systems
Recirculating pumps should not be used for filling and emptying pools as there is a danger that they might harbour bacteria. The same hose should never be used to fill and empty the water to avoid contamination. (See Appendix, page 180 for further details.)

Waterproof immersion heaters are ideal and should be used only when the mother is *not* in the pool. Heat can be retained with a heat retention cover. Thermostats are not necessary if there is a thermometer.

Locating the Pool
Ideally, the pool should be situated in a place where semi-darkness, privacy, intimacy and seclusion can be ensured and there is close proximity to a toilet. The mother should choose a part of the house where she feels she would most like to give birth, bearing in mind her need for privacy (see page 99). There should be enough room for the birth to take place on the floor beside the pool as well.

On a practical level it is important to ensure that the floor can support the weight of the pool. If you are in any doubt, then it is advisable to get a structural engineer to come in and advise you (they can be found in the yellow pages or the telephone directory). It is not necessarily essential for the pool to be on the ground floor, but it must be on the same level or below the water supply.

When locating the pool in the room choose the strongest part of the floor – i.e. in a corner or bay window or over a load bearing wall on the floor below.

For information and details about setting up a portable pool, see Appendix on page 180.

INSTALLING A POOL IN HOSPITAL
Hospital pools have become much more sophisticated since Michel Odent first introduced an inflatable children's pool into the birthing room at Pithiviers.

Fibreglass water birth pools of excellent design are now available for permanent installation in hospitals (see page 183). There are also hospital pools on wheels which can be moved from one suite to another and the portable pools described in the previous section can be hired or purchased by parents or the hospital and easily used in the birth suite.

The most suitable designs for use in hospital are circular, oval or eliptical (see page 163). Installing a plumbed-in pool is very simple and requires no more maintenance than a large bath.

Most hospitals can take the weight of such a pool which is essentially a large bath and is full for only a few hours at a time. It is usually not necessary for the pool to be on the ground floor.

The Pool Room

The pool should be installed in a room as large as a medium-sized bathroom, preferably with its own toilet adjacent to the pool. A room which is too large will not feel sufficiently intimate or private. There must be enough room for birth to occur beside the pool rather than in the water, if necessary. There should also be a wash basin. A hand-held power shower attached to the pool is a useful option to provide hydrotherapy massage or silent filling during labour.

When choosing the decor for the room, natural earthy tones and the use of plants and cushions can help to make the room as attractive, comfortable and homelike as possible. The presence of a toilet will help the mother to feel free to empty her bowels or pass urine, giving her a sense of privacy and safety so that she can allow her body to open and release without inhibition or the inconvenience of having to leave the room. Some mothers find sitting on the toilet is comfortable before and during the first part of the second stage, and close proximity without having to walk across a corridor is ideal.

The floor of the pool room should be covered in an easily-cleaned non-slip material. Portable steps help the mother to enter and leave the pool and they can be used as low stools.

The needs and comfort of the midwife and birth attendants are important. Bean bags, low chairs or stools are very useful for this purpose and allow the attendants to be comfortable without towering over and watching the mother in the pool. Other items needed in the birth room are listed on page 164 under 'Essential Equipment'.

Sterility

The surfaces of the pool room and the pool itself should be easily cleanable with antiseptic detergent used in hospitals.

For portable pools a disposable liner is an essential prerequisite and this is thrown away at the end of each birth. Birth pools require the same attention as a normal bath either at home or in hospital.

Lighting

The lighting in the room is very important indeed. Dimmer switches on the lights and curtains or blinds at the window provide the optimum dark environment for privacy and relaxation in labour. Fluorescent lights should be avoided. Visibility beneath the surface of the water is easily attained by using a submersible torch. These float on the surface of the water, provide a low light and are usable beneath the surface. However, with experience, it is usually not necessary to see the vaginal outlet and the general lighting level in the room will suffice to observe the birth. The sounds the mother makes in the second stage of labour will make the birth of the baby obvious (see page 106) and the midwife can use her hands to feel what is happening if she needs to.

Pool Size and Shape ·
The rounded contours of circular, oval or eliptical pools are best suited to creating the womb-like feeling conducive to birth. They take up less room than a circular pool and have several advantages. They provide a secure space at the narrow end for the mother to lie back and feel contained and comforted, and easier access for the midwife. There is a smaller volume of water and thus less stress on the joists and the structure of the hospital itself. There is adequate length and width allowing the mother to use a wide range of positions with enough room for the midwife to deliver the baby and for the partner to enter the pool if necessary.
Length: The pool should be a minimum of 5½ feet (1.7m) long so that the mother can float completely freely in the water.
   The side walls of the pool should in the main be vertical so that the woman can hold on to the rim and squat or kneel in comfort. Another advantage of an oval shape is that one of the sides could be sloped, thus making a comfortable place for the mother to recline, particularly in the first stage of labour.
Width: In an oval pool the mother can lie across the width of the pool and use her feet to press against the sides if she wants to. A good width is approximately 4 feet (1.2m).
Depth: The water level must be a minimum of 24 inches (60 cm). This will cover the abdomen when the mother is kneeling or squatting. It is helpful to have this depth of water in order to provide sufficient buoyancy for the woman in the pool.
   The rim of the pool should have a rounded contour if possible, in the shape of a hand rail a minimum of 1½ inches in diameter. This provides a surface for the woman to hold on to, particularly in the second stage of labour, in order to facilitate the birth. The pool should be sufficiently strong for the partner or birth attendant to be able to sit on while supporting the pregnant woman either in or outside the water. A vertical pool side allows greater ease for the birth attendant to support the mother from inside or outside the pool. If the pool is installed on the same level as the floor, there should be a wide plug hole so that the pool can be drained easily and quickly without the plug becoming blocked with debris.
   There should also be a variety of plastic-covered pillows that can be used by the woman in the water. They are useful for resting her head and to have something under her knees if she spends a lot of time kneeling.

ESSENTIAL EQUIPMENT NEEDED FOR A WATER BIRTH

- An efficient portable room heater which can heat up the birth room rapidly.
- A large strainer or sieve and bucket for removing debris.
- A digital thermometer for testing the water temperature. These are available from chemists and, if used at home, can be used later for your baby.
- Plenty of towels and one extra kept warm for the baby.
- A towelling bath robe.
- A low stool or two for partners, birth attendants and to assist getting in and out of the pool. The plastic variety can be used both in and beside the pool.
- Non-slip surface – a large non-slip bath mat is ideal and can be used later when bathing with your baby.
- A comfortable chair and a beanbag or pile of cushions.
- A space on the floor prepared with bath mats laid down, for use if the mother prefers to leave the pool.

TEMPERATURE

The room should be kept at a temperature which is comfortable for the woman in labour. This is often several degrees lower than that which is necessary later for the baby. If the water or room temperature is too high the mother may be unable to sweat and lose heat in the humid atmosphere. There is a risk that the mother will become overheated and exhausted.

If the baby is born in water the room should be comfortably warm. When the baby's breathing is established the room temperature needs to be increased before mother and baby leave the pool. The pool room should include an effective heater in addition to central heating facilities, so that the temperature can be raised rapidly soon after the birth.

Water Temperature

The temperature of a large body of water changes very slowly. Maintaining the correct water temperature is important and easy to do. Fathers often enjoy monitoring and maintaining the temperature of the water. The water temperature should be kept around body temperature between 95°F and 101°F (35°C – 37°C). If it is too low the mother's body temperature, particularly if she spends a long time in the pool, will drop. The sweating mechanism for heat loss does not work in water, so if the water is too warm the mother's body temperature will rise and her energy may be sapped. Obviously if the mother is feeling cold, additional hot water should be added to the pool. The water temperature can be assessed intuitively by using your elbow, as you would test a baby's bath water.

The mother's temperature can be checked every few hours to make sure that it is being maintained. This is especially important if she spends a prolonged period of time in water. While the average length of time spent in the water is one to two hours, it is not unusual for women to stay in the water pool for over four hours during the course of a labour.

At the moment of birth and during the immediate postnatal period, the baby's temperature should be maintained. Additional warm water may need to be added. If the water temperature is appropriate then the mother's temperature will be normal and at the same time her skin will absorb water, thus minimising any dehydration which may occur as a result of a diminished fluid intake during labour.

USING THE POOL

The pool is useful in the days preceding the birth, during labour, for the birth itself or in the hours and days thereafter. The way in which women and their partners use the pool varies according to individual needs and what is most appropriate at the time. Guidelines as to when and how to use the pool and how long to stay in the water are given in chapter 5 (Labour and Birth).

Monitoring the Baby's Heartbeat

It is wise to monitor the foetal heart immediately before the mother enters the pool. It is simple to perform intermittent foetal heart monitoring while she is in the water. If she is floating on her back it is easiest to ask her to come to the surface so that the baby's heartbeat may be monitored by using a manual Pinnard Stethoscope or a hand-held electronic foetal heart monitor. The skin can easily be dried and the transducer of the foetal heart monitor then placed on the mother's abdomen. If this is done immediately after a contraction, then the important type II decelerations can be detected. Electronic foetal heart monitors may be used under water for intermittent or continuous monitoring. Telemetry systems allow the heart beat to be counted by a microphone held on the mother's abdomen sending signals to the monitor a few yards away.

If the mother is on her hands and knees or in the squatting position, then the foetal heart may only be audible below the surface of the water. The older types of electronic foetal heart monitor can be used under water. The transducer can be smeared with jelly to conduct the sound waves and then wrapped in a single or double condom in order to keep it watertight. It is essential, as the condom is pulled over the transducer, to expel all the air so that the interface consists of transducer, conducting jelly and condom sheath. This can then be applied directly onto the mother's abdomen under water. The one difficulty with this type of monitoring is water damaging the transducer if the condom bursts. The same transducer wrapped in a condom can be used for external monitoring if the woman decides to come out of the water.

In normal labour foetal heart monitoring should be performed every 30-60 minutes early in the first stage and more frequently as the labour progresses. In the second stage of labour it is possible to monitor the baby's heartbeat frequently with minimal inconvenience to the mother so that the baby's well-being is kept in focus throughout.

Examinations
Monitoring of the mother's temperature and pulse can easily be done in or out of the water. Blood pressure is recorded prior to entering the pool or by asking the mother to sit on the rim. Monitoring the mother's temperature ensures that she is not over or underheated.

Abdominal examinations are simple in water. A vaginal examination can easily be performed in the water with the mother lying, kneeling or squatting, or supported by her partner. Occasionally it is mechanically difficult for the midwife or doctor if the mother is squatting. In this case the midwife has to bend over the pool, put her hand and arm under the water as far as the shoulder. Provided the midwife has a flexible back this is easy to do (see page 172 for exercises for the midwife). If the water pool has been sterilised prior to the birth or has a new pool liner there is minimal risk of the introduction of infection to the mother as the result of a vaginal examination. Theoretically fewer organisms from the mother's external genitalia will be introduced during a vaginal examination in water than would be introduced if it were performed on land (see page 168).

Visibility and Access
Water birth is essentially a 'hands off' technique. If the mother is kneeling, lying or floating in the water it is easy to see the external genitals and observe the birth. In the squatting position the side of the pool sometimes obscures the midwife's vision. An underwater light and a mirror aid visibility but are usually unnecessary because the midwife can assess what is happening by feel.

Access by birth attendants to the labouring woman and the baby depends on two factors: their relationship with the pregnant woman and the design of the birth pool. If the relationship is a close one then it is easy to ensure that the birth occurs near enough to the edge of the pool or alternatively, the midwife may very rarely have to actually get into the water. If the midwives attending a waterbirth wear light cotton trousers that can easily be changed should they get wet, entering the pool at short notice is simple. The midwife should be ready to do this in an emergency but it is very seldom necessary, and most midwives do not enter the pool. Some pools are specially designed to make access to the woman easy from all around.

Protecting the Perineum, Tears and Episiotomy
Midwives who practise active birth with minimal intervention and relinquish control wherever possible gain confidence in assisting birth in a variety of postures (squatting, kneeling, lying or standing) and a variety of situations using a bed or the floor or birth stool. As experience with active birth increases the transition to water birth becomes easy.

The experienced midwife places her hand on the baby's head as it begins to emerge and to crown. In some hospitals mothers are encouraged to do this themselves and ther is a notable reduction in tearing. It is very easy, with practice, to feel the degree of stretch and give in the vaginal tissues. Water softens the skin and allows it to stretch so that deep tears are very uncommon under water. With experience it becomes progressively less important to constantly watch or touch the perineum or to interfere with the spontaneity of birth.

If the mother chooses to lie and float, the perineum can easily be protected if necessary. If squatting is the preferred mode of delivery, visibility may be more limited. Under these circumstances the midwife's hands placed on the baby's head will allow the midwife to feel the perineum. The squatting position makes the baby's descent and delivery easiest and assistance by the midwife is rarely needed. Provided that there is no feeling that the birth should be hurried, gradual delivery of the baby's head is perfectly easy and possible with minimal stretching or tearing of the tissues. The watery environment will allow the skin to expand to a greater extent than normal and the weightlessness will reduce the external pressure on the mother's vaginal tissues. If tears do occur during a water birth it is very unusual for them to be extensive. It is common to find superficial lacerations or a slightly deeper tear in the perineum in the midline which are simple to repair. This can be done at leisure on land after the birth has been completed, the placenta has been born and the baby welcomed into the world. Episiotomy is rarely necessary with birth in water, but when needed the vagina and perineum can be incised with the mother floating on her back or kneeling.

It is safe for the mother to get back into the water again after stitching.

Birth Under Water
During the second stage the wellbeing of mother and baby is easily observed by traditional midwifery practice and monitoring. Low lighting and a warm secure atmosphere encourage the normal physiology of birth. Monitoring the baby's heart beat is easy to do even when the lighting is low. The temperature and seating arrangements in the pool room are important to aid the comfort of midwives and birth partners. Direct eye-to-eye contact and looking down on the labouring woman are best avoided.

Depending on the position the mother chooses, the head may crown in full view and visibility. Alternatively the midwife may use her hand to gently feel the crowning. With experience minimal intervention is needed. Crowning and birth of the head does not need to be hurried. When the baby's head is born it is preferable to wait for the next contraction which may take 2-3 minutes. At this time the birth attendants need to remain calm. The baby may open her eyes under the water. The pulsation of the umbilical cord and perfusion of the baby from the placenta continues throughout this time. The birth of the baby's body occurs with the next contraction. Usually no intervention is needed as the body is born spontaneously. Occasionally, gentle traction of the baby's head will assist the birth. Slow birth of the shoulders minimises tearing of the vagina and perineum. The umbilical cord, after the birth of the shoulders, is protected by gently easing the baby's body into the pool. The baby does not float spontaneously and gently sinks to the bottom of the pool. The pulsation of the cord continues and can easily be checked whatever the mother's position. Bringing the baby to the surface too hastily may cause excessive traction on the umbilical cord and even cause the cord to rupture. The tension on the umbilical when the midwife holds the baby's body may be greater than expected. It is not necessary to feel for the umbilical cord prior to the birth of the shoulders once the head is out. The baby will be born with the following contraction, and feeling for the cord is extremely uncomfortable for the mother. Even if the cord is around the baby's neck it is simple to rotate the baby's body under the water immediately after birth and disentangle it. Cutting the cord prior to the birth of the shoulders is risky, time-consuming and unnecessary.

The baby should be brought above to the surface of the water within a minute of the birth of the umbilicus and held turned face down to allow the amniotic fluid to drain from her mouth and air passages. The baby now breathes and is gently handed to her mother. The baby's trunk is supported on the midwife's forearm with her hand under the chest. Keeping the baby underwater for a prolonged period is dangerous. There is a failsafe mechanism where the placenta continues to perfuse the baby with oxygen during the first minutes after birth while breathing is stabilised. Suction of the nose and air passages is rarely needed, but can be done, if needed with the baby resting on the mother's chest. Advanced neonatal resuscitation requires clamping of the umbilical cord and moving the baby to a resuscitaire.

The third stage of labour consists of greeting the baby and observing the miracle of a new life. There is no need to hurry and the cord may pulsate for up to 30 minutes and need not be clamped. The next uterine contraction may occur within 5-15 minutes and will bring with it separation of the placenta. The normal bonding process which occurs at this time between mother and baby includes the first sucking and stimulates the onset of uterine contractions. The routine use of syntometrine is not indicated. Delivery of the placenta may occur in the pool if it is easy. The mother may elect to squat or kneel for this stage of labour. If there is excessive bleeding or a feeling of faintness the mother should be helped to leave the pool.

The Baby Inhaling Water

Many parents and attendants are concerned about the possibilty of the baby inhaling water at the moment of birth. When the head emerges underwater the chest is in the mothers's pelvis and water cannot be inhaled because the lungs do not expand. The stimulus for the baby to breathe is contact with the cold air and this only occurs when the baby is brought to the surface of the water. During birth the baby is nourished and oxygenated by the placenta and there is no risk of inhalation if the baby is brought to the surface soon after birth.

The baby will only begin to breathe once his body comes into contact with the atmosphere. If the mother stands up at the moment of birth and the baby is born above the water surface, the midwife should deliver the baby outside the water and pass him directly to her. In this case, the baby may take his first breath immediately after birth and for this reason the head should not be re-immersed in the water (see photographs on page 130).

There is no possibility of either mother or baby drowning in the birth pool, provided that there are birth attendants present. This is a deep-seated, yet unrealistic, anxiety in some people who have a fear of water. Provided the baby is gently lifted out of the water in the first minute or so after the birth there is no risk of inhalation of water. After the birth the baby's body may remain immersed after breathing is well established with the head and face above the water surface.

Shoulder Dystocia
In the unlikely event of the shoulders being difficult to deliver the midwife leans into the water and applies traction to the baby's head to help the front shoulder under the pubic bone. If this is ineffective the mother changes position and is helped into a standing squat and supported from behind so she can use maximal downward force to expedite the birth (see page 112). She may have to leave the pool to maximise the help of gravity.

Body Excretions
Birth in the pool will result in the passage of urine, faeces and blood into the water. The amount of urine passed is usually minimal and this is rapidly diluted into a large volume of water and will not affect the baby at birth. It is very easy to remove faecal debris by using a household strainer and plastic bucket. This is particularly easy to do if there is a toilet in the room. The amount of faecal material lost at birth does not tend to be large and the practicalities of this are simple. After the birth the water is sometimes tinged with blood. A small volume of blood will discolour the water because of the rapid diffusion of the red blood cells throughout the entire volume of water in the pool and parents should be prepared for this. Occasionally, blood clots in the vagina are passed into the pool. These are of no consequence to mother or baby and can be scooped up with a strainer or, if they are small, passed through the plug hole. There is no need to empty the pool if amniotic fluid, blood, urine or faeces enter the water since risk of infection is minimal.

Risk of Infection

Mother and Baby
A pregnant mother's skin and vagina always have organisms which are satellite to her body. These are present throughout life and only become pathogenic or harmful if the mother's natural immunity or resistance is altered in some way. The baby has antibodies from the mother and is adapted to her organisms. Being born into a pool of water containing these organisms is safe.

It is usual for excretions from the mother's body to enter the water but the incidence of infection is not increased after waterbirth.

If the water pool has not been adequately cleaned or there are bacteria in the water supply, obviously an additional source of infection can be introduced into the pool. Emptying the pool completely and disinfecting after each use makes the risk of infection no greater than taking a bath, which many mothers do after birth.

If the membranes have ruptured, then the protection of the amniotic sac in preventing the migration of organisms from the upper vagina into the amniotic fluid is removed. If rupture of membranes is prolonged, i.e. over 24 hours, there is a theoretical risk of amniotic and foetal infection. This risk is increased by vaginal examinations introducing organisms from the outside environment, including the mother's external skin, into the vagina. It is likely that being in water actually reduces this possibility. It is unnecessary to prevent a woman whose membranes have ruptured from using the birth pool since the vaginal walls will prevent water from entering the cervix or uterus. Likewise a vaginal examination can be performed in the pool in relative safety, provided due care and attention is paid to cleansing the pool between births. If the membranes have ruptured, internal examinations should be avoided unless essential.

The Midwife
HIV and Hepatitis virus can theoretically infect medical attendants but there is as yet no known example of water-borne infection from the HIV (AIDS) virus. The highest risk is when the mother is a carrier of the virus and her blood comes into contact with an open wound in the skin of the birth attendant, or where there is accidental puncture of the skin by a needle, thereby possibly carrying the infected blood into the midwife's deep tissue. If infected blood is passed into the pool, then the viruses come into contact with the water of the pool and water will reduce but may not negate the infectivity.

Nevertheless, there is a risk to birth attendants and it may become necessary to screen all women who wish to use the pool for labour and birth for HIV or Hepatitis. At the present time birth attendants overcome this risk with the use of rubber gloves. In some hospitals longer rubber gloves are used so that midwives can safely put their arms into the pool.

Bleeding and Haemorrhage
The amount of blood lost during and after delivery is difficult to estimate if the woman is in water. The amount of blood looks greater in the pool and estimates would then err on the side of caution. Clinical experience with water births is very important with regard to this. If the bleeding seems excessive then the woman should leave the water immediately so that this can be more accurately assessed and dealt with. The third stage of labour can then continue outside the pool.

Water Embolism
This is an unlikely, theoretical risk of introducing water into the uterus as the placenta is born which would, in theory, allow water to enter the mother's bloodstream through the blood vessels at the placental site. With increasing

experience of water birth it is obvious that this is not a practical risk.

In 1983, Michel Odent raised the question of water entering the vagina and the uterine cavity if the placenta is delivered while the woman was still in water. Since that time many water births have occurred and many placentae have been born into the water without any incidence of water embolism. In reality, immediately after birth, the vaginal walls touch one another even if there is a tear so that the vagina is a potential cavity rather than an actual one. The placenta is malleable and has the consistency of liver. When it is born from the lower vagina, the walls of the upper vagina have already come together, thus making it extremely unlikely that any water could reach the uterine cavity.

Risk of Injury in and out of the Water

So long as the mother is never left unattended in labour there is no risk of the mother injuring herself in the pool or when getting out.

Careful attention to non-slip surfaces both on the bottom and also outside the pool, adequate towelling facilities, a low stool to step onto, adequate facilities for heating the pool room on getting out of the water, are all useful in preventing accidents. Particular attention is essential after birth as women can feel faint in the first six hours. These are all issues that become second nature when a midwife is familiar with the use of a water pool in labour.

In the rare instances when the mother actually faints in the water then two people are needed to help her out and they need to step into the pool. It will help if her partner is in the pool to lift her. The mother should be held under the armpits by two people and helped out of the water. Then she should be placed flat on the floor, or on a bed, with her legs elevated to get the blood to circulate to her head and revive her. Her head should be turned to the side if she vomits.

CONTRA-INDICATIONS TO THE USE OF WATER

First Stage of Labour

In the first stage of labour there are relatively few contra-indications to the use of water.

- The main one is if the mother doesn't want to be in water.
- If the baby requires continuous foetal heart monitoring because there is evidence of hypoxia, meconium in the amniotic fluid or if there is a high possibility of foetal distress. Meconium usually rises to the water surface and can be easily seen. Continuous monitoring using telemetry is now available for use under water without rupturing the membrane.
- Antepartum haemorrhage with excessive bleeding.
- Severe pre-eclampsic toxaemia with excessively high blood pressure and the possibility of eclampsia.

The vast majority of women are able to use the birth pool quite safely for pain relief in labour provided progress is satisfactory.

Second Stage of Labour
- Twin pregnancy with all the attendant possible obstetric complications.
- Babies who are in the breech position, destined for vaginal delivery, should, as a rule, be born on land. With a breech baby there is a fixed time interval between the birth of the umbilicus and the birth of the head because the baby's chest compresses the cord against the side wall of the mother's pelvis and there is minimal blood flow in the cord. Ideally, no longer than five minutes should elapse between the birth of the umbilicus and the birth of the head. In order to expedite birth the use of the upright position, particularly the upright supported standing squat position (see page 112) on land provides maximum help from the downward force of gravity to assist the expulsive reflex and birth of the baby.
- If a baby is extremely premature it will need assisted respiration or intensive care facilities immediately after the birth and the birth should take place in a more conventional labour ward with adjacent facilities.
- When foetal distress occurs during labour, it is possible that the baby will require resuscitation and birth should not take place in water. The main sign of distress is alteration of the foetal heart tones. The administration of oxygen and resuscitation is obviously easier if birth occurs adjacent to the resuscitation equipment. Also, the help of gravity in upright positions will be necessary so the baby can be born as soon as possible.
- Prolonged second stage when the use of gravity and upright posture on land will expedite the birth.

Third Stage of Labour
- If the delivery of the placenta is delayed, the mother should leave the water.
- In the presence of heavy vaginal bleeding or where there is a significant risk of postpartum haemorrhage, the third stage of labour should be completed on land.
- If the baby needs resuscitation or oxygenation the mother should leave the pool.
- If the mother feels faint she should leave the pool or the water should be drained.

Postnatal
There are virtually no contra-indications to the use of water postnatally. In the immediate postnatal period, i.e. one to six hours after birth, there is a risk of the mother feeling faint, particularly if the labour has been long or if there has been excessive bleeding during the birth. Very careful attention should be paid to the temperature of the water and there should be attendants present to assist the mother as she comes out of the water to prevent her injuring herself. This is an important safety issue.

Most babies are very happy to have their first bath within minutes or hours of being born. This depends, however, on the state of well-being of the baby. If there are any breathing problems or problems with temperature control for the baby then obviously this needs to be postponed.

It is possible and enjoyable to breastfeed while in the water (see page 145) and provided the temperature of the water and of the birth pool is well controlled then there is no risk of the baby's temperature becoming hypo or hyperthermic (see page 164).

CARING FOR THE MIDWIFE'S BACK

The presence of a birth pool in labour implies that the midwife will spend time either kneeling or sitting adjacent to the pool. If the midwife suffers from back problems these can be exacerbated. It is, however, quite therapeutic to either kneel or squat on a low stool because, over a period of months, this strengthens the midwife's lower back muscles and will, in the long term, improve her posture. There are a few basic exercises that midwives might consider doing in order to improve their posture and the strength and flexibility of the spine.

These postures and exercises will help the midwife and may be of important long term benefit to her. The incidence of back problems among nurses in general is very high and building up the back muscles and improving the flexibility and tone in the spine is of great benefit.

The water exercise programme in chapter four is as beneficial for midwives as it is for pregnant mothers. Exercising in water with the mothers you are going to attend is an excellent way to establish trust and security. Taking up yoga is one of the best therapies for general health and can improve your posture and the condition of your spine permanently. It is also very relaxing, meditative and centring and a great help for midwives and mothers alike.

Try to be conscious of the way you stoop to lift up a heavy object or support a mother in labour (see page 174).

With a little careful thought and good postural habits, stress on the spine can almost always be avoided.

Exercises to strengthen Midwife's back

Lying on the Back and Pelvic Lift
With bare feet, lie on your back on the floor with your knees bent. If it is more comfortable you can place a book under your head. Your feet should be about twelve inches apart and parallel, with heels close to your buttocks. Place your arms by your sides with the palms face down. Breathe deeply and feel the way your back contacts the floor. Relax your shoulders and lengthen your neck by dropping your chin towards your chest. Tuck your pelvis under, so that your lower back lengthens and the back of your waist touches the floor. Lie like this and breathe for about five minutes before you start and do this whenever you are tired. (Lying down on your back for a while is marvellously therapeutic, even if you don't do anything else in the way of exercise.)

To begin the pelvic lift, exhale, and at the same time drop your heels, lengthen your lower back and lift your pelvis slowly, keeping neck and shoulders relaxed. Inhale while up and continue breathing. Hold for a few moments.

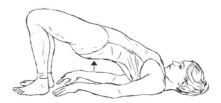

Pelvic lift

Now exhale and come down very slowly, lowering your spine on to the floor one vertebra at a time from the neck downwards until your lower back completely releases on to the floor.

Repeat this four to six times slowly and then hug your knees gently to your chest with your arms to release your lower back.

Spinal Twist
Still lying on your back, spread your arms out to the sides at the height of your shoulders. Bend both knees and bring them up towards your chest with ankles together. Breathe and relax. Now turn your head and look at your left hand. Exhale and turn slowly to the right, bringing your knees towards the floor so your spine rotates gently. Go only as far as you can without straining and keep your shoulders and arms on the floor. Breathe and relax like this for a few moments and then come to the centre and repeat on the other side. When you find this easier you can hold the top thigh with the opposite hand.

Spinal twist

All Fours Tuck-In (not illustrated)
Kneel on the floor with your hands and knees twelve inches apart. Exhale and lengthen your lower back down towards your heels so that your pelvis tucks under and your back arches. Inhale and relax, returning to the resting position. Repeat ten times.

Forward Bend
With bare feet, stand with your feet twelve inches apart and parallel and toes spread apart. Drop your weight down into your heels. Drop your lower back down towards your heels. Now bend forward slowly from the hips allowing your trunk to hang forward loosely like a rag doll. Relax your neck and shoulders and let your head hang. Stay in this position with your knees straight and breathe deeply. As you exhale, feel your hamstring muscles at the back of your legs stretch and lengthen. Hold for a few minutes concentrating on long, slow, releasing out-breaths, and then come up slowly. Regular practise will lengthen your hamstring muscles creating better mobility in the hip joints so that there is less stress on the lower back when you bend forward. (When the hamstrings are tight, the bend comes from the lower part of the spine rather than the hip joints, resulting in back ache.)

Forward bend   Supported forward bend

If your back is very stiff, then try placing your palms on a table when you bend forward, keeping your arms and elbows straight so your trunk forms a right angle to your legs. This is easier as your back is supported.

Positions to Use When Attending a Mother in the Pool

Sitting
Use a low stool when sitting next to the pool. Squat down with your feet and knees apart and parallel. Lower your pelvis on to the stool and relax your lower back by lengthening it down towards the stool. Keep your spine straight.

Squatting often will help to improve and strengthen your back.

Kneeling
Kneel on a soft surface with your knees slightly apart and your feet turning inwards. You may find it more comfortable to place a cushion or two between your buttocks and your calves. Relax your lower back by lengthening it down towards your heels as if you have a long tail, going down.

Bending
Try to avoid unnecessary bending. When you do, place your feet apart and parallel. Keeping your knees slightly bent, bend forward from your hip joints keeping your spine as straight as possible. If this is difficult, then try kneeling on a low stool instead.

Lifting
Always bend your knees or squat rather than stooping to lift a heavy object.

Supporting in a Squat
When supporting the mother in a standing squat make sure you bend your knees and lean *back* so her weight is supported by your pelvis and thighs rather than your back. Keep your shoulders and arms relaxed.

If you have a bad back, then use the partner squat on page 113 or sit on a chair with the mother squatting between your legs. Educate fathers to do the supporting instead of you wherever possible.

PARENTS' RIGHTS IN ARRANGING A WATER BIRTH
We are grateful to Beverley Lawrence Beech of AIMS for her advice in this section. More information may be gained from her book *Who's Having Your Baby?*, and from the AIMS leaflet on Water Birth (see page 189).

Arranging a Water Birth at Home
It is usually most constructive to seek a midwife to attend your home birth in the first instance. If you are looking for a community midwife then the first step is to write to the Supervisor of Midwives in your area, informing her that you intend to have your baby at home and will be having a water pool as an option for use during labour and birth. Ask her, if possible, to allocate a midwife to you who is experienced in, or enthusiastic about, waterbirth. Tell her that you take full responsibility for your decision to have your baby at home and to use a water pool.

Legally, you have the right to give birth at home in water with or without the approval of a GP or obstetrician, provided a midwife attends the birth. Midwives are obliged to come by law if you call them when in labour. You may find that while some midwives welcome the idea of waterbirth, others may be apprehensive, inexperienced or untrained. This is understandable, since labour and birth under water may be new for the midwife.

A midwife who feels inadequately trained to deliver babies in water is legally entitled to refuse to do so. It is the responsibility of the superintendent of midwives to find you a suitable midwife.

There are also independent midwives who are happy to deliver babies at home in or out of water and the Independent Midwives Association or the Association of Radical Midwives may be helpful (see useful addresses).

Arranging a Water Birth in Hospital or GP Unit

This may be more difficult than arranging to have a water pool at home. Some hospitals already have a birth pool and many more are likely to follow suit in the future. Hospitals in the UK known to have one at the time or writing are listed on page 182.

Theoretically you have the right to approach any hospital for your birth, and if you persist you may find that you will be accepted. Some hospitals may allow you to bring in a hired pool. The best way to go about this is to book directly with the midwives by writing to the Director of Midwifery Services at the hospital. Inform her that you would like to have your baby at the hospital and to bring in a portable water pool as a option for use during labour and birth, and ask her to make the necessary arrangements.

You may find that the hospital engineers and various other experts have to be consulted about safety and technicalities, and sometimes this can be the stumbling block.

If you run into problems arranging for a waterbirth at home or in hospital, AIMS advises the following tactics:

- If midwifery or medical staff object, then bypass them and write to the Unit General Manager and seek his/her help. They are often very sympathetic.
- Ask the midwifery or medical staff to advise you *in writing* of their objections.
- Ask them to provide scientific evidence to support their objections or criticisms.

If none of this works, AIMS suggests that you contact them immediately for guidance and support (see page 188). The basic principle is that it is your body, your baby and your birth. Medical and midwifery attendants are advisors. They are there to help, support and advise you and while they have every right to give you advice, you do not have any legal or other obligation to take it.

MIDWIFES' AND OBSTETRICIANS' LEGAL ISSUES

Litigation and Insurance

During the past decade there has been a dramatic increase in the number of litigation cases and law suits brought by the public against doctors and nurses. The steepest rate of increase is in obstetrics. Obstetricians and midwives are now categorised as being in the highest insurance risk category. The number of claims for injuries sustained by babies during childbirth rose exponentially during the past five years to a crisis point. At the beginning of 1990 a crown indemnity scheme was introduced whereby doctors and midwives working within the National Health Service were protected for their work on NHS patients by the crown indemnity. That is, the state has undertaken to meet the expenses of any legal costs incurred as a result of damage during childbirth. This has been extended and will now include coverage of doctors in all disciplines for NHS work. Doctors and midwives employed exclusively in private practice, or partially in private practice, will have to have additional medical insurance to cover this aspect of their work.

When a labouring woman is in water she is still defined as being in normal labour. There is no conflict with the guidelines given in the Midwives' Code of Practice and no reason to fear legal complications, so the use of water for labour and birth should present no additional legal problems. In fact, most midwives' concerns about using water for labour and birth are more to do with midwifery practices than legal issues and these are dealt with in detail earlier in this chapter and in chapter five.

REFERENCE LIST

Chapter 1
1. Inch, Sally, *Birth Rights*, Green Print, 1989
2. Roberts, Joyce, 'Maternal Position During the First Stage of Labour', *Effective Care in Pregnancy and Childbirth*, Chalmers, Enkin and Kierse, Vol. 2:55 page 883 Oxford University Press, 1989
3. Balaskas, Janet, *New Active Birth*, Unwin Paperbacks, 1989
   Balaskas, Janet and Gordon, Yehudi, *The Encyclopaedia of Pregnancy and Birth*, Macdonald Orbis, 1987
4. Naaktegeboren, Cornelis, 'The Biology of Childbirth' *Effective Care in Pregnancy and Childbirth*, Chalmers et al, Vol. 2:48 page 795 (see ref. 2)
5. Odent, Michel, 'The Fetus Ejection Reflex', *Birth* (USA) 14: June 1987
6. Sidenbladh, Erik, *Water Babies*, Adam and Charles Black, 1983
7. Leboyer, Frederick, *Birth Without Violence*, Fontana, 1983
8. Leboyer, Frederick, *A Child is Born*, film made with Pierre Marie Goulet
9. Odent, Michel, *Birth Reborn*, Souvenir Press, 1984
10. Odent, Michel, 'Birth Under Water', *Lancet*, December 1983, 24/31
11. Daniels, Karil, *Water Baby Information Book*, Point of View Productions, San Francisco, USA, revised 1988
12. Naaktegeboren, Cornelis, (see ref. 4)
13. Reference sources for information on cetacea:
    1 Williams, Heathcote, *Whale Nation*, Jonathan Cape Ltd, 1988
    2 Encyclopeadia Britannica
    3 *Whales, Dolphins and Porpoises of the Pacific*, from 'Shorelines of America' series, K.L. Publications, Nevada, USA, 1985
    4 Williams, Heathcote, *Falling for a Dolphin*, Jonathan Cape Ltd, 1988
    5 Anderson, K., *Whales, Dolphins and Porpoises*, Inter-continental Publishing Ltd, Hong Kong, 1988
14. Nollman, Jim, 'Dolphin's Dreamtime', *Talking to the Animals*, Anthony Blond, London 1985
15. Dobbs, Horace, *Follow a Wild Dolphin*, Souvenir Press, 1990
16. Cochrane, Amanda and Callen, Karena, *Dolphins and their Power to Heal*, Bloomsbury, 1992
17. Sidenbladh, Erik, *Water Babies* (see ref. 6)
18. Odent, Michel, *Water and Sexuality*, Arkana, 1990
19. Hardy, Alister, 'Was Man More Aquatic in the Past?', *New Scientist*, Vol 7 (April 1960), pp642-5
20. Morgan, Elaine, *The Aquatic Ape*, Souvenir Press, London 1982
    The Descent of Woman
21. Griscom, Chris, *Ocean Born*, Wilhelm Goldmann Verlag, Munchen (Germany)

Chapter 2 (sources)
Lovelock, J.E., *Gaia*, Oxford University Press, 1979
Gwynn, Richard, *Way of the Sea*, Green Books, 1987
Cirlot, J.E., *A Dictionary of Symbols*, Routledge, 1988
Cooper, J.C., *An Illustrated Encyclopaedia of Traditional Symbols*, Thames & Hudson, 1978
Encyclopaedia Britannica
Guyton, A.C., *Textbook of Medical Physiology*, Chapter 1, W.B. Saunders & Co, 1986
Sadler, T.W., *Langmans Medical Embryology*, Williams and Wilkins, 1985

Chapter 3
1. Balaskas, Janet, *New Active Birth*, Unwin Paperbacks, 1989
    Balaskas, Janet and Gordon, Yehudi, *The Encyclopaedia of Pregnancy and Birth*, Macdonald Orbis, 1987
2. Roberts, Joyce, from *Effective Care in Pregnancy and Childbirth*, Chalmers, Enkin and Kierse, Vol. 2:55, page 883 Oxford University Press, 1989
3. Simkin, Penny, 'Stress, Pain and Catecholamines in Labour', *Birth*, (USA) 13: pages 227-233
4. Simkin, Penny, 'Non-Pharmacological Methods of Pain Relief in Labour', *Effective Care in Pregnancy and Childbirth*, Chalmers et al, Vol. 2:22 page 895 (see ref. 2)
5. Odent, Michel, 'The Fetus Ejection Reflex', *Birth* (USA), 14: June 1987
6. Brown, C., 'Therapeutic Effects of Bathing During Labour', *from J. Nurse Midwifery*, Vol. 27, pages 13-16, 1983
7. Simkin, Penny, 'Non-Pharmacological Methods of Pain Relief in Labour', (see ref. 4)
8. Odent, Michel, 'Birth Under Water', *Lancet* ii, pages 1976-7, 1983
9. Rosenthal, Michael, 'Water Birth: An American Experience', from *Water Baby Information Book*, Daniels, Karil, Point of View Productions, San Francisco, USA, revised 1988
10. Rosenthal, Michael (see ref. 9)
11. Odent, Michel (see ref. 8)
12. Brown, C. (see ref. 6)
13. Rosenthal, Michael (see ref. 9)
14. Odent, Michel (see ref. 8)
15. Odent, Michel (see ref. 8)
16. *Health Committee Report on Maternity Services – House of Commons* (page xcviii, para 327), H.M.S.O. Publications Centre, London, February 1992

Appendix

HOW TO SET UP A PORTABLE POOL

Portable pools may be used at home or in a hospital and can be set up and emptied very quickly. However, it may take several hours to get the pool filled with water at the correct temperature, depending on the availability of hot water. It is advisable to set up the pool prior to, or as soon as, labour begins, to ensure that it will be ready by the time the mother needs to use it.

Floor Surface

Place a large sheet of thick plastic from your local do-it-yourself store on the floor where the pool will be located. If the floor surface is not carpeted and the pool is of the double liner type, place a suitable padding under the plastic sheet to provide a soft ground surface for the mother in labour. A firm one inch foam cut to the size of the base of the pool is ideal, or else blankets can be used. Put the pool in place assembling all parts securely. If liners are being used, make sure they are correctly in place before filling the pool. Make sure that any padding is in the right position as you cannot change this once the pool is filled with water.

Filling the Pool

Remember to have a dress rehearsal before the day of the birth. You will need two hose pipes: one for filling the pool, and a separate one for emptying the water once it has been used. It is important that you ensure beforehand that you have the right type of fitting to attach the hose onto your taps or you could be dealing with a flood!

Once filled, the pool is usable for a birth for the next 24 hours. After this the water will need to be changed. Ordinary tap water can be used without any additives, although some people add salt to increase the salinity of the water to match that of amniotic fluid (1 tablespoon per gallon).

a   *Continuous hot water supply*

If there is a continuous hot water supply you will not need a water heater and can simply use hot and cold water from the taps.

Fill the pool so that it is slightly warmer and slightly less deep than you will eventually need it. Then cover it with a heat retention cover which should be supplied with the pool. If a cover is not available, a substitute can be made using thick bubble wrap from a swimming pool supply store. Cut this to shape to fit just inside the pool rim. (Wash the cover in the bath with a mild household disinfectant and rinse thoroughly prior to use).

When the mother wishes to enter the pool, take off the cover, adjust the temperature and depth by adding hot or cold water and the pool is then ready for her to use. If the pool is too full, use a bucket rather than the pump to empty it a little, or use a hose to top it up if it is too shallow for her comfort.

b *Boiler System*

Most homes have a boiler and cylinder which hold approximately 30 gallons of hot water. In this case, you will certainly need a heating system and pump supplied with the pool. Before you start, set your boiler on high to get the water as hot as possible. You will need to fill the pool and heat the water in phases. If your pool is the double liner type, start by filling the base with cold water. This will enable you to use your hands to smooth out any creases in the liner as the water comes in so that there is a smooth surface for the mother to kneel on. Then add as much hot water as you can. Fill the pool to drain the immersion heating system so that it can be turned on to begin reheating the water. Cover with the heat retention cover and wait for the boiler to heat up again. Add the hot water from the boiler to the pool with the hose and repeat this procedure until the pool is filled with warm water, a few degrees warmer than you will need (see page 164). Cover until the mother is ready to use it.

The pool should never be filled any higher than 4 inches below the rim or it will spill over when the mother enters the water.

Once the pool is filled and covered, take all pumps and heaters out of the room so that it is not cluttered with technical equipment. The water can be heated later by using the hose to add more hot water from the tap.

Heating the Water

If you have an ordinary household boiler you will need a water heater. This should be an electrical immersion heater for heating liquids and not a recirculating system with a pump. The latter heats and recirculates the water from the pool and is not suitable for use with birth pools as bacteria and germs from the used water could build up in the system. **The mother should not be in the pool when any type of electrical heater is in place, even if the manufacturer says it is safe.**

The water should be heated to temperature before the mother enters the pool and a heat retention cover should be used if it is ready for use. This will keep the water to temperature, losing approximately 1° per hour. It is easy to raise the temperature when the mother needs the pool by adding hot water from the household system. (See page 164-5 for details about water temperature.)

Emptying the Pool

Ideally, a portable pool should come with an electrical water pump. There are two types – one which is submersible and one which stands outside the pool. The submersible variety is more efficient and can empty the pool within ten minutes. Make sure all fixtures are secure and that the hose which carries the outflow leads into a bath tub or drain which can handle the quantity of water rapidly coming out (bathroom or kitchen sinks are not adequate). Before turning on the pump remove any solid debris with a strainer.

When drained, a one-piece pool can be washed and flushed out with water and disinfectant. In the double liner variety you simply throw away the inner liner. If you wish to re-use it you will need to clean it in the bath with disinfectant. Clean and dry thoroughly all parts of the pool and return it on time as someone else is probably waiting for it!

Water Birth Resources

Active Birth Centre
55 Dartmouth Park Road,
London NW5 1SL

071 267 3006 (tel)
071 267 5368 (fax)

The Centre is run by Janet Balaskas and her husband Keith Brainin who is the designer of the Aqua Pool range of portable and installed birth pools. These can be used in hospitals or at home and are available for hire or purchase. Pools can be shipped anywhere in the U.K.

The Active Birth Centre also offers workshops and lectures on Water Birth and a comprehensive programme for expectant and new parents as well as a mail order catalogue and current list of water birth facilities throughout the U.K.

HOSPITALS WITH WATER POOL FACILITIES

At the time of publication there are approximately 30 hospitals, both NHS and private, with an installed water pool in Great Britain, and the number is increasing steadily. Many others are willing to accommodate parents who hire a pool themselves and bring it into hospital for the duration of their birth.

An up-to-date list of hospitals with water birth facilities and pool hire companies can be obtained by sending an S.A.E. to the Active Birth Centre (see above).

WATER AND BIRTH RESOURCE LIST

This list is up to date at the time of publication. For more recent contacts, pool brochure or further information write to the Active Birth Centre (see below).

Oxford Sonicacid Ltd
Quarry Lane
Chichester
W. Sussex PO19 2LP
0243 775022
FM7, Foetal monitor suitable for use under water.

International Water Birth Contacts

Austria
Geburtshaus Nussdorf
Contact Michael Adam MD
Heiligenstadterstrasse 217
A-1190 Wien
Austria
(011) 43 1 374937

Australia and New Zealand
c/o Estelle Myers
PO Box 111 Kings Cross
Sydney 2011 NSW
Australia

The Hawthorn Birth and Development Centre
Contact J. Sutherland
144 Barkers Road
Hawthorn
Victoria
Australia
(011) 61 3 819 2088

Belgium
Contact Dr. Ponette
Gerstraat 1
8400 Ostende
Belgium

H. Serruys State Hospital
Contact Dr. Ponette
Ostende
Belgium
32 59 707 637

Versalius Hospital
Contact Dr. Van Coppenolle
Brasschaat (Antwerp)
Belgium
32 3 651 5000

Denmark
Gentofte Amts Hospital
Contact Elizabeth Feder – Head of Maternity
Niels Anderson Vej. 65
2900 Hellerup
Copenhagen
Denmark
(011) 45 1 65 1200

Finland
Aktivinen Synntys
c/o Anne May Sulonen
Kieritkalen 21
SF 39110 Simuna – Finland

France
Centre Hospitalier Generale
45300 Maternité
Pithiviers
France
(011) 33 38 301 049

Maternité des Lilas
Contact Dr Peterman
14 Rue du Coq Francaise
Les Lilas
France
(011) 331 4360 0265

Japan
Waterbirth Project Group
88-24 Kamata, Shizouka,
Shizouka-Japan 421-01

Malta
Dr Josie Muscat
St. James Natural Birth Centre
Zabbar
Malta
(011) 824699

Russia
U/Rustaveli 15A-61
Moscow
Russia
219 5937
Contact Igor Tjarkovsky

South Africa
333 Gallo Manor
Sandton 2052
Johannesburg
South Africa
802 2964
Contact Caryl Misselbrook

Spain
Acuario
c/Manuel Candela 9
46021 Valencia
Spain
Contact Drs Pedro Enquix and Enrique Lebrero

Sweden
Swedish Childbirth Association
c/o Janette Brandt
Heidenstamsgarten 41
75427 Uppsala

Switzerland
Christina Hurst-Prager
Mooswiesstrasse 9
9122 Pfaffhausen
Switzerland
411 825 1245

Julia Jus
Bahnhofstrasse 15
6403 Kuessnacht am Rigi
Switzerland
41 960964

USA and Canada
For a comprehensive resource list of midwives, doctors and birth centres throughout the USA, Canada and internationally, and also to obtain the video *Water Baby* by Karil Daniels, write to Karil Daniels, Point of View Productions, 2477 Folsom Street, San Francisco, CA 94110, (415) 821 0435.

Family Birthing Center
1125 E Arrow Highway
Upland
CA 91786
USA
(714) 946 7001
Contact Michael Rosenthal MD

Water Birth International
PO Box 554
Sanata Barbara
California 93150

USEFUL ADDRESSES

The Active Birth Movement
55 Dartmouth Park Road
London NW5
Tel. 071 267 3006   Fax 071 267 5368

Association for the Improvement in Maternity Services (AIMS)
40 Kingswood Avenue
London NW6 6LS   081 960 5585

Association of Radical Midwives (ARM)
62 Greetby Hill
Ormskirk
Lancashire L39 2DT

Independent Midwives Association
65 Mount Nod Road
Streatham
London SW16 2LP

International Homebirth Movement
22 Anson Road,
London N7 ORD

National Childbirth Trust
Alexandra House
Oldham Terrace
Acton
London W3 6NH

Royal College of Midwives
15 Mansfield Street
London W1

Society to Support Home Confinements
17 Laburnum Avenue
Durham

Products

Active Birth Centre Catalogue (Mail Order)
55 Dartmouth Park Road
London NW5 1SL
071 267 6745
Ready-made pure aromatherapy, pregnancy, labour and baby care oils and products. Also books by mail order and baby carriers.

Water and Birth — the Video
This is a 48-minute inspirational video made by Janet Balaskas and Amy Hardie, featuring the water births of three women and interviews with their midwives. It is available by mail order from the Active Birth Centre.

Waterproof Foetal Heart Monitors
These can be obtained from Oxford Sonicaid Ltd (see page 183)

Essential Oils by Post
Aroma-Therapy Supplies
Unit W3
The Knoll Business Centre
Old Shoreham Road
Hove, Sussex BN3 7GS
0273 693622

RECOMMENDED READING

Water during Birth and Infancy
AIMS, leaflet on Water Birth (see Useful Addresses)
Balaskas, Janet, *New Active Birth*, Unwin Paperbacks, 1989
Daniels, Karil, *The Water Baby Information Book*, Point of View Productions, USA
Daniels, Karil, *The Water Baby Video*, Points of View Productions, USA
Hawley, Anne, *Swim Baby Swim*, Pelham Books, 1984
Odent, Michel, *Birth Reborn*, Fontana, 1986
Odent, Michel, *Water and Sexuality*, Arkana, 1990
Sidenbladh, Erik, *Water Babies*, Adam & Charles Black, 1983
Walker, Peter & Fiona, *Natural Parenting*, Bloomsbury, 1987

General
Balaskas, Janet and Gordon, Yehudi, *The Encyclopaedia of Pregnancy & Birth*, Macdonald Orbis, 1987
Balaskas, J. and A., *New Life, The Exercise Book for Childbirth*, Sidgwick & Jackson, 1983
Balaskas, J., *The Active Birth Partner's Handbook*, Sidgwick & Jackson, 1984
Balaskas, Janet, *Natural Pregnancy*, Sidgwick & Jackson, 1990
Balaskas, J., *Yoga for Pregnancy*, audio cassette and booklet available from Active Birth Centre
Beech, Beverley, *Who's Having your Baby?* Camden Press, 1987
Flint, Caroline, *Sensitive Midwifery*, Heinemann, 1986
Inch, Sally, *Birthrights*, Hutchinson, 1982
Junor, Viki and Monaco, Marianne, *Homebirth Handbook*, Souvenir Press, 1987
Kitzinger, Sheila, *Freedom and Choice in Childbirth*, Penguin, 1988
Odent, Michel, *Primal Health*, Century, 1986
Walker, Peter, *Baby Relax*, Unwin Paperbacks, 1986
Walker, Peter, *The Book of Baby Massage*, Bloomsbury, 1988
Wesson, Nicky, *Alternative Maternity*, Optima, 1989
Wessen, Nicky, *Home Birth*, Optima, 1990
Williams, Heathcote, *Falling for a Dolphin*, Jonathan Cape, 1988
Williams, Heathcote, *Whale Nation*, Jonathan Cape, 1988

Index

Note: bold figures denote illustrations or photographs